AF860544

AN

HISTORICAL SKETCH

OF THE

LAW OF COPYRIGHT;

WITH

REMARKS ON SERGEANT TALFOURD'S BILL:

AND

AN APPENDIX

OF THE COPYRIGHT LAWS OF FOREIGN COUNTRIES.

BY JOHN J. LOWNDES, Esq.

With a new introduction by Ronan Deazley

Reader, Birmingham Law School, University of Birmingham

THE LAWBOOK EXCHANGE, LTD.
Clark, New Jersey
2008

ISBN-13: 978-1-58477-912-4
ISBN-10: 1-58477-912-8

The quality of this reprint is equivalent to the quality of the original work.

THE LAWBOOK EXCHANGE, LTD.
33 Terminal Avenue
Clark, New Jersey 07066-1321

Please see our website for a selection of our other publications and fine facsimile reprints of classic works of legal history:
www.lawbookexchange.com

Library of Congress Cataloging-in-Publication Data

Lowndes, John James, b. 1814.
An historical sketch of the law of copyright : with remarks on Sergeant Talfourd's bill, and an appendix of the copyright laws of foreign countries / by John J. Lowndes ; with a new introduction by Ronan Deazley.
p. cm.
Originally published: London : Saunders and Benning, 1840.
Includes bibliographical references.
ISBN-13: 978-1-58477-912-4 (cloth : acid-free paper)
ISBN-10: 1-58477-912-8 (cloth : acid-free paper)
1. Copyright. 2. Copyright--Great Britain. I. Talfourd, Thomas Noon, Sir, 1795-1854. II. Title.
Z589.L88 2008
346.04'82--dc22

2008041283

Printed in the United States of America on acid-free paper

INTRODUCTION[1]

I

Since the passing of the *Statute of Anne* 1710, determining the appropriate duration of the copyright term for literary (and other) works has provided a point of perennial controversy and debate. The 1710 Act set out that new works were to be protected for fourteen years, with an additional period of fourteen years if the author was still alive at the end of the first term.[2] Throughout the mid-eighteenth century, however, a considerable body of law and literature was devoted to the question as to whether the statute had created new rights in relation to the printing and publishing of literary works, or whether the legislation simply served to complement a pre-existing common law copyright in those works. These debates culminated in the two landmark decisions of *Millar* v. *Taylor* (1769)[3] and *Donaldson* v. *Becket* (1774).[4] In *Millar*, a divided King's Bench, led by Lord Mansfield, concluded that copyright was a creature of the common law and as such lasted in perpetuity; the statutory periods of protection laid down in

---

1. This commentary draws upon work developed for an AHRC-funded digital archive project: *Primary Sources on Copyright (1450-1900)*; for further details, see: www.copyrighthistory.org.
2. Statute of Anne, 1710, 8 Anne, c.19, s.1. In addition, works already in print were to receive a twenty-one year term of protection commencing on 10 April 1710; ibid.
3. *Millar* v. *Taylor* (1769) 4 Burr 2303.
4. *Donaldson* v. *Becket* (1774) 4 Burr 2408, 2 Bro PC 129.

the legislation did not affect the substance or duration of the common law right, but simply delineated the times within which one might claim the statutory penalties for the infringement of the same. The boon that authors and publishers enjoyed as a result of *Millar* was, however, cut short in *Donaldson* when it was decided by the House of Lords that, whether copyright existed at common law or not, the duration of copyright in published material was definitely limited to the periods of protection set out within the statute.[5]

Forty years after *Donaldson*, the term of protection for literary works was amended by the *Copyright Act* 1814, which provided that copyright would last for a single twenty eight year term after which "if the author shall be living" the work was to be protected "for the residue of his natural life".[6] This guaranteed lifetime interest was not, however, to the satisfaction of all. Five years after the new legislation

---

5. The exact nature of the decision in *Donaldson* still remains a matter of some controversy. For relevant commentary see: H. Abrams, "The Historic Foundation of American Copyright Law: Exploding the Myth of Common Law Copyright", *Wayne Law Review*, 29 (1983): 1119-91; R. Deazley, *On the Origin of the Right to Copy: Charting the Movement of Copyright Law in Eighteenth-Century Britain (1695-1775)* (Oxford: Hart Publishing, 2004), 191-220; M. Rose, *Authors and Owners. The Invention of Copyright* (London: Harvard University Press, 1993), 92-112; J. Whicher, "The Ghost of Donaldson v Beckett: An Inquiry into the Constitutional Distribution of Powers over the Law of Literary Property in the United States", *Copyright Society of the USA*, 9 (1961-62): 102-51, 194-229.
6. Copyright Act, 1814, 54 Geo.III, c.156, s.4. Nor was this the first time that a lifetime interest had been suggested by the legislature – that first occurred in 1737; for details see: Deazley, 103-108.

came into force, Robert Southey, then poet laureate, wrote in the *Quarterly Review*:

> The question is simply this: upon what principle, with what justice, or under what pretext of public good, are men of letters deprived of a perpetual property in the produce of their own labours, when all other persons enjoy it as their indefeasible right – a right beyond the power of any earthly authority to take away?[7]

Of concern to Southey was that, without a post mortem term of protection, an author's family might be "deprived of the property, just when it is beginning to prove a valuable inheritance". He continued: "Restore to [authors] that perpetuity in the copyright of their works, of which the law has deprived them, and the reward of literary labour will ultimately be in just proportion to its deserts".[8]

7. R. Southey, "Inquiry into the Copyright Act", *Quarterly Review*, (1819): 196-213 (211).
8. Ibid., 213. Southey had previously written, in similar terms, about the iniquity of the duration of the copyright term in a review of Isaac D'Israeli's *Calamities of Authors*. Writing before the passing of the 1814 Act, Southey noted that "[a]s the law at present stands, an author may retain or dispose of the property of his works for a term of eight and twenty years, after which it becomes common property". He continued: "Upon what principle of common equity or common sense has such a law been founded? And why is it that those persons who, of all others, confer upon their country the most lasting honour and the most permanent benefit, should be the only ones to whom the state denies a fee simple in the produce of their own industry?" R. Southey, "D'Israeli's *Calamities of Authors*", *Quarterly Review* (1812): 93-114 (111).

Five years after Southey, when the essayist Joseph Lowe wrote the entry on 'Copyright' in the supplement to the sixth edition of the *Encyclopædia Britannica*, much of his commentary was similarly given over to the question of the copyright term.[9] Like Southey, Lowe favoured a perpetual term of copyright protection for all authors;[10] on the other hand, he was also of the opinion that neither the public, nor the legislature, would sanction the introduction of such a term – at least, not without "the clearest proof of public advantage" in relation to the same. Indeed, the mistake of the London book trade in the mid-eighteenth century, he suggested, lay "in demanding perpetuity instead of prolongation".[11] Rather then press for a perpetual copyright, Lowe proposed that the copyright term for literary works be extended to fifty years; he continued, however, that during the last twenty-two years of that term, should the owner of any copyright work "withhold publication, or

9. M. Napier, ed., *Supplement to the fourth, fifth and sixth editions of the Encyclopædia Britannica*, 6 vols (Edinburgh: Constable & Co, 1824), 3: 328-38. As with Southey, Lowe had previously written on the subject, again within the context of a review of D'Israeli's *Calamities of Authors*, when he argued that "a prolongation of the term of copyright would lead to the attainment of a most desirable result, - the substitution of a moderate number of good books for an almost countless quantity of such as are bad". J. Lowe, "D'Israeli's *Calamities of Authors*", *The Monthly Review*, 2nd ser., (1813): 248-57 (257).
10. Lowe wrote that "[p]erpetuity of copyright is as much the right of the author or purchaser of a book, as of the builder or purchaser of a house; and the public will never reap its full harvest of advantage from literary composition till the law be made to confirm the claim of equity"; Lowe, "Copyright", 333.
11. Ibid., 330.

confine [publication] to an expensive form", a specially appointed copyright commission would have the authority to order the publication of the same and at a reasonable price.[12] This, in Lowe's opinion, would address any concerns the public might have about extending the term. Moreover, with this safeguard in place, he argued that an extension would only operate to the benefit of authors, publishers, and the public alike.[13] All that was needed, Lowe concluded, was that the question be "taken up by a spirited and persevering member of Parliament".[14]

Lowe's call for a parliamentary champion would be answered just over a decade later when, in the late 1830s, Thomas Noon Talfourd, M.P. for Reading, took up the cause of copyright reform.[15] Between 1837 and 1841 Talfourd strove, in vain, to restructure and revise the law of copyright, before losing his parliamentary seat in the general election

---

12. He wrote as follows: "Grant, in all books to be hereafter published, a prolongation of copyright for twenty-two years, making in the whole fifty years. Appoint a commission (with power of reference to a jury) to act in all cases where the owners of copyright withhold publication, or confine it to an expensive form. Empower this commission to order the publication of such works, in the form which they judge most proper, and without any other obligation towards the proprietor of the copyright than that of paying over to him or his representatives the proportion of profit accruing, by the practice of the trade, to the owner of a copyright"; ibid., 334.
13. Ibid., 334-37.
14. Ibid., 337.
15. Between the publication of Lowe's commentary and the commencement of Talfourd's campaign to reform the law of copyright, various other writers argued the case for an extended copyright term; see for example: R. Maugham, *A Treatise on the Laws of Literary*

of 1841. The following year, Lord Mahon (Philip Henry Stanhope) took up where Talfourd left off; by contrast with his predecessor, he was successful in securing the *Copyright Act* 1842.[16] Between the start of Talfourd's campaign, and the conclusion of the same by Mahon, two editions were published of the first British treatise specifically dedicated to the history of copyright: John James Lowndes' *An Historical Sketch of the Law of Copyright*.[17] Born in 1814, Lowndes was called to the bar in 1833 and became a barrister to the Inner Temple. In addition to publishing on copyright, he was the author of a controversial pamphlet, *A Few Brief Remarks on Lord Denman's Bill for Improving the Law of Evidence*,[18] and contributed to a number of law reports throughout his professional career.[19]

Property (London: 1828); J.K.A., "Literary Property", *American Jurist and Law Magazine* (1833): 62-81 (78-80).

16. Copyright Act, 1842, 5&6 Vict., c.45. The genesis of, and background to, the Copyright Act 1842 has been exhaustively discussed by Catherine Seville in her book on *Literary Copyright Reform in Early Victorian England: The Framing of the 1842 Copyright Act* (Cambridge: Cambridge University Press, 1999).

17. J.J. Lowndes, *An Historical Sketch of the Law of Copyright* (London: Saunders and Benning, 1840). See also Maugham's *Treatise* which does include a lengthy section providing an 'Historical View of the Law'; Maugham, 1-62.

18. J.J. Lowndes, *A Few Brief Remarks on Lord Denman's Bill for Improving the Law of Evidence* (London: Saunders and Benning, 1843).

19. See for example: A.S. Dowling and J.J. Lowndes, eds, *Reports of cases argued and determined in the Queen's Bench Practice Court*, 7 vols (London and Dublin: Sweet, 1845-51); J.J. Lowndes and P.B. Maxwell, eds, *Bail Court Cases*, 4 vols (London: Sweet, 1852-1854).

II

When Talfourd brought the first of his copyright Bills before the Commons in June 1837, his initial intention had been to codify the various strands of existing domestic copyright legislation within one statutory measure.[20] In addition, this Bill proposed to put the issue of the rights of foreign authors (as well as works first published outside the British dominions) upon a legislative footing.[21] The draft Bill, however, proved to be overly ambitious. The government of the day made it clear that the issue of international copyright relations was an inappropriate subject for a back-bench initiative; indeed, moves were already afoot on a government measure that would address the same.[22] Talfourd capitulated,

20. *Bill to consolidate and amend the Laws relating to Copyright in Printed Books, Musical Compositions, Acted Dramas and Engravings, to provide Remedies for the Violation thereof, and to extend the Term of its Duration*, 6 June 1837, Paper No.380, I: 573. This Bill did not however attempt a complete codification of the copyright regime in that it didn't incorporate the existing copyright legislation relating to works of sculpture.

21. During the 1820s and 1830s, the question of what rights a foreign author had under the British copyright regime increasingly came before the courts; in general see: R. Deazley, *Rethinking Copyright: History, Theory, Language* (Cheltenham: Edward Elgar Press, 2006), 42-55. To address this Talfourd proposed that should an author register their work within one year of publication outside the British dominions, and thereafter publish the work within the British dominions, then they were to "have and enjoy the Copyright thereof within the dominions of His Majesty for the like term, commencing from its first publication"; 1837 Bill, clause 11.

22. On 20 March 1838, the government introduced a Bill that would

and in December 1837 sought leave to bring in a revised Bill which, when presented to the Commons on 28 February 1838, confined itself to domestic copyright issues only, and only in relation to literary, dramatic and musical works.[23] Like its predecessor, it failed to progress beyond the Committee Stage in the Commons. In 1839, 1840 and 1841, three more Bills were introduced, each of which confined itself to the same basic parameters of Talfourd's 1838 Bill, and each of which failed to pass the Commons.[24]

The issue that was singularly responsible for the five year controversy surrounding Talfourd's proposals concerned his plans to extend the existing copyright term; as Seville writes: "[b]y the time that the 1842 Act was finally passed, it was widely regarded as a single-issue piece of legislation".[25] Talfourd sought to introduce a term that would last for the life of the author plus sixty years after his or her death and, despite the considerable protestations which his

result in the passing of the International Copyright Act, 1838, 1&2 Vict., c.59, which Act provided that the British monarch could, by Order in Council, grant copyright protection, within Britain and its Dominions, to the authors of literary works first published abroad for a period specified within the Order but not exceeding the domestic copyright term.

23. *Bill to amend the Law of Copyright*, 27 Feb. 1838, Paper No.164, I: 489; see also *Bill to amend the Law of Copyright*, 6 June 1838, Paper No.461, I: 505.

24. See: *Bill to amend Law of Copyright*, 12 Feb. 1839, Paper No.19, I: 505; *Bill to amend Law of Copyright*, 11 Feb. 1840, Paper No.61, I: 415; *Bill to amend the Law of Copyright*, 29 Jan. 1841, Paper No.6, I: 429.

25. Seville, 18.

proposed term engendered,[26] he refused to compromise upon the same. Only when Lord Mahon took over from Talfourd in 1842 was the proposed term of protection reduced to the life of the author plus twenty-five years. Even this proved controversial and was defeated in the Commons by a vote of 68 to 56.[27] However, upon the suggestion of Sir Robert Peel, then Prime Minister, Mahon's proposal was modified again to a single forty-two year term, or the life of the author plus seven years post-mortem, whichever was longer. When Peel's proposal was comprehensively carried by a vote of 91 to 33, the fate of Mahon's Bill seemed assured.[28]

The timing of the publication of Lowndes' work owes everything to Talfourd's efforts to reform the law of copyright. The first edition was published early in February 1840 just as Talfourd introduced the fourth of his unsuccessful Copyright Bills.[29] The second edition was published in April 1842 as Lord Mahon's Bill was passing from the Commons to the Lords for consideration and debate. Both were dedicated to Talfourd "[f]or his generous

26. The opposition to Talfourd's proposals came from a number of quarters. Between 1838 and 1840 nearly 500 petitions were lodged in parliament objecting to the proposed legislation. Publishers, printers, and radical politicians such as Thomas Wakley and Henry Warburton, marshalled a variety of arguments that touched upon questions of free trade, the freedom of the press, and the significance of cheap literature to the encouragement and spread of popular education; in general, see Seville.

27. Hansard, 3rd ser., 61 (1842): 1397.

28. Ibid., 1398; *Journal of the House of Commons*, 97 (1842): 165.

29. The Preface to the first edition of Lowndes' treatise is dated 31 January 1840. Talfourd sought leave to introduce his fourth *Copyright Bill* on 4 February 1840; Hansard, 3rd ser., 51 (1840): 1250.

advocacy of the rights of authors". Moreover, in his prefatorial remarks to both, Lowndes made clear the extent to which his work was designed to supplement and support Talfourd's cause. For Lowdnes, the object of the book was "to give a succinct historical account of the origin of property known as 'Copyright' and of the modifications and alterations it has subsequently undergone down to the present time". As for his "motive in laying it before the public", it was an attempt "to remove the misapprehensions which prevail with regard to this species of property, both as to its former existence, and as to the effect and expediency of the measure proposed by Sergeant Talfourd".[30]

III

The treatise itself is, essentially, a work in two halves, the first of which is concerned with tracing the history of copyright from the invention of printing until the passing of the *Copyright Act* 1836.[31] Like Talfourd, Lowndes was convinced that the concept of an author's natural right of

30. Lowndes, vii.

31. Copyright Act, 1836, 6&7 Will.IV, c.110; this Act reduced the number of copies of new works that publishers had to be deposit with the Stationers' Company for the benefit of certain public libraries from eleven to five. For further commentary, see: R. Deazley, "The Life of an Author: Samuel Egerton Brydges and the *Copyright Act* 1814", *Georgia State University Law Review*, 23 (2007): 809-46; J. Feather, "Publishers and Politicians: The Remaking of the Law of Copyright in Britain 1775-1842, Part I: Legal Deposit and the Battle of the Library Tax", *Publishing History*, 24 (1988): 49-76; J.C.T. Oates, "Cambridge University and the Reform of the Copyright Act, 1805-

literary property was one of long-standing, and that copyright existed at common law prior to the interventions of the legislature in the guise of the *Statute of Anne* 1710. With his treatise, he sought to convince the reader of the same.[32] The prerogative grants of the Tudors that concerned printing were, for Lowndes, "proof of the recognition of literary property", just as the Elizabethan injunctions of 1559 and the subsequent Star Chamber Decree of 1566 were both "in favor of Copyright".[33] The passing of the 1710 Act did not evidence an absence of common law rights, but rather "was sought to render [the author's] right more beneficial, by the remedy being made more effective".[34]

Lowndes covers the first three hundred years of his history in just forty pages of text, after which follows a

1813", The Library, 5th ser., 27 (1972): 275-92; D. McKitterick, Cambridge University Library, A History: The Eighteenth and Nineteenth Centuries (Cambridge: Cambridge University Press, 1986), 394-445; and, R.C.B. Partridge, *The history of the legal deposit of books throughout The British Empire* (London: The Library Association, 1938).

32. In the Preface to the first edition, Lowndes wrote that "more time and study than have been in my power to bestow, are necessary to do justice to this subject, but if, by the perusal of the following pages, the reader is convinced that such a right as that known by the name of Copyright did formerly exist at common-law, and was only taken away by a mistaken interpretation of the effect of the statute of Anne, and that the state of the present law is such as imperatively demands alteration; I shall not consider the few leisure hours I have appropriated to their composition from the severer duties of my profession, as either misspent or unprofitably employed".

33. Lowndes, 2, 5, 14.

34. Ibid., 32.

fifteen page treatment of *Millar*, the decision in which "the nature, custom, and law of literary property were most fully and ably discussed".[35] *Donaldson*, not surprisingly perhaps, does not receive the same level of attention as *Millar*. Certainly, as a decision of the House of Lords it was "esteemed practically decisive of the point"; however, it was also presented to the reader as a decision lacking "sound construction",[36] and one about which the Court of King's Bench, in the subsequent decision of *Beckford* v. *Hood* (1798),[37] "could not conceal from themselves, the injustice of such a construction, or reconcile it to the language of the act". Moreover, the decision in *Beckford* itself, in which the court held that a copyright owner did not have to register his or her work in order to seek damages for infringement of the same, was for Lowndes further evidence that the 1710 Act "did not take away the author's pre-existing common-law right".[38]

The second part of the book was given over to the more recent past in that Lowndes provides an account of and commentary upon the first three Bills that Talfourd had already presented before the Commons (in 1837, 1838 and 1839).[39] In relation to his history of Talfourd's efforts to

35. Ibid., 41.
36. Ibid., 58, 100.
37. *Beckford* v. *Hood* (1798) 7 D&E 620.
38. Lowndes, 62.
39. In the Preface to the second edition, Lowndes updated his work by including some brief commentary upon the Copyright Bills that Talfourd introduced in February 1840 and in January 1841, and upon Lord Mahon's endeavours in relation to the Bill that would become the 1842 Act.

secure new legislation, much of the commentary simply involves verbatim transcripts of the arguments that Talfourd himself presented in the Commons in relation to the same. Indeed, within this part of the treatise, nearly half of the text is taken up with extracts from Talfourd's contributions to the parliamentary debates.[40] So it is that we get Talfourd's thoughts on the "reward due to an author", on "those who seek to deprive genius of all substantial reward", and upon "the injustice of the term of Copyright being dependent on the author's life".[41]

Following this, Lowndes concludes the second half of his work by offering some general observations about the substance of Talfourd's proposals, while at the same time addressing some of the objections raised by those who argued that the proposed extension of term would be "profitless to the author, indifferent to the publisher, and injurious to the public". Extend the term, he suggested, and England could no longer be reproached as "the tardiest nation in according justice to authors".[42] Interestingly, however, while Lowndes

40. Lowndes, 80-83, 86-89, 94-97.

41. Ibid., 80, 81, 86.

42. Ibid., 100, 105. Noting that the "term of Copyright is greater in almost every other country than in England", Lowndes, in an Appendix to his treatise, provided some commentary upon the term of copyright protection that had been adopted for literary works in a number of foreign countries, including the US, France, Holland, Spain, Russia, and a number of the states that made up the German Confederation. One reviewer considered the material in the Appendix to be of particular value, noting that it was "full of important knowledge as to the law of copyright abroad; and proves, that if Englishmen have the character of being liberal, it is not in the patronage of the literati of their own country"; *The Mirror*, 35 (1840): 155.

agreed with the principle of term extension, he disagreed with Talfourd as to the appropriate length of that extended term. "It is not at all clear", he wrote, "that the extension of the Copyright should be to exactly sixty years from the death of the author; indeed, as a matter of opinion, I am inclined to think that two-thirds of that period, or perhaps even less, would be sufficient".[43]

We know that it was the duration of Talfourd's preferred copyright term that proved to be the single most significant stumbling-block in his unsuccessful campaign to reform the law of literary copyright. We also know that Lord Mahon had read Lowndes' treatise shortly after it was first published, and considered it a work "worthy of the greatest attention".[44] One is left to wonder what role Lowndes' comments on the copyright term might have played in contributing to Mahon's decision to reduce the post-mortem term from sixty to twenty-five years when he introduced the first draft of the 1842 Bill to the Commons. Had Mahon not reduced the term, the Bill might simply have suffered the same fate as Talfourd's 1841 Bill which failed to progress beyond a second reading.[45] On that occasion, Thomas Babington Macaulay had famously lambasted copyright as a "tax on readers for the purpose of giving a bounty to writers", and an "evil [that] ought not to last a day longer than is necessary for securing the good",[46] before having Talfourd's Bill thrown out.[47] By

43. Lowndes, 106.
44. Hansard, 3rd ser., 52 (1840): 411.
45. Hansard, 3rd ser., 56 (1841): 341-60.
46. Ibid., 348, 350.
47. On the day on which the 1841 Bill received its second reading, William Gladstone, who had supported and advised Talfourd in his

contrast, when Mahon introduced the 1842 Bill, Macaulay pronounced it "a great improvement on that of last year" and, while he continued to object to the inclusion of a post mortem term,[48] he was nevertheless hopeful that, after five years of wrangling, the Commons might be able "to arrive at a satisfactory measure".[49] As it was, Peel's proposal on the copyright term was adopted and the *Copyright Act* 1842 was finally secured.

Ronan Deazley
September 2008

efforts, noted in his diary: "Copyright bill thrown out by 45 to 38. Macaulay *did* it"; M.R.D. Foot & H.C.G. Matthew, eds, *The Gladstone Diaries, vol.III (1840-47)* (Oxford: Clarendon Press, 1974), 82.

48. When Peel suggested that a seven year post mortem term be included to ensure that an author was in a position "to provide for his family after death", Macaulay objected on the basis that, if provided with a single forty-two year term "a prudent man ought to be able to make some provision for his children, [whereas] to give a term after death was rather offering an encouragement to expenditure"; Hansard, 3rd ser., 61 (1842): 1394.

49. Ibid., 695.

AN

HISTORICAL SKETCH

OF THE

LAW OF COPYRIGHT;

WITH

REMARKS ON SERGEANT TALFOURD'S BILL:

AND

AN APPENDIX

OF THE COPYRIGHT LAWS OF FOREIGN COUNTRIES.

BY JOHN J. LOWNDES, Esq.

LONDON:

SAUNDERS AND BENNING, FLEET STREET.

1840.

AN

HISTORICAL SKETCH

OF THE

LAW OF COPYRIGHT.

PRINTED BY J. GREEN AND CO., BARTLETT'S BUILDINGS, LONDON.

TO

SERGEANT TALFOURD, M.P.,

&c., &c., &c.,

FOR HIS GENEROUS ADVOCACY OF THE RIGHTS OF AUTHORS,

The following Pages

ARE, WITH MUCH RESPECT, BY PERMISSION,

DEDICATED.

PREFACE.

THE object of the following little treatise is to give a succinct historical account of the origin of the property known as 'Copyright,' and of the modifications and alterations it has subsequently undergone down to the present time.

The motive in laying it before the public, is to attempt to remove the misapprehensions which prevail with regard to this species of property, both as to its former existence, and as to the effect and expediency of the measure proposed by Sergeant Talfourd.

It will be seen by the Appendix, that in almost every country but Great Britain, Copyright is continued for some period after the author's death, for the benefit of his heirs; and yet a Bill for this purpose has been for three sessions before the British legislature, and each session postponed: and this, owing not so much to any opposition existing to its principle, which has been each time affirmed by respectable majorities, as to the apathy with which every question is treated, which does not awaken the spirit of party, or touch the ever-sensitive chord of self-interest; and which has thus suffered an insignificant minority to defeat it in detail.

I feel sensibly that more time and study than have been in my power to bestow, are necessary to do justice to this subject; but if, by the perusal of the following pages, the reader is convinced that such a right as that known by the name of Copyright did formerly exist at common-law, and was only taken away by a mistaken interpretation of the effect of the statute of Anne, and that the state of the present law is such as imperatively demands alteration; I shall not consider the few leisure hours I have appropriated to their composition from the severer duties of my profession, as either mispent or unprofitably employed.

J. J. L.

INNER TEMPLE,
January 31st, 1840.

HISTORICAL SKETCH

OF THE

LAW OF COPYRIGHT.

CHAPTER I.

FROM THE INVENTION OF PRINTING, TO THE FORMATION OF THE STATIONERS' COMPANY IN 1556.

To seek the origin of Copyright in times prior to the invention of Printing, would partake more of curious research than of useful investigation, and would, at best, furnish rather matter of conjecture than of information. In the following pages, therefore, we shall confine our inquiry as to the commencement of this right, to the evidences afforded by the regulations and customs respecting the first printed books; which, seeing the scanty materials that are handed down to us, we shall find to be a work involving sufficient doubt and uncertainty, without occupying our time by a search into darker or more remote periods.

It is improbable, that even in the Augustan age, an age rich in literature and the arts, any such right ever existed.* How much more difficult then must it be to show, that in

* But copies appear to have been sold for the purpose of recital before an audience. See Prolog. in Eunuch. Terentii, 20; Mart. Epigr. i, 67, iv, 72, xiii, 3, xiv, 194; Juv. vii, 83. But this, doubtless, implied no exclusive right.

the rude and troubled times which preceded the introduction of printing into this country, a custom of Copyright obtained here. And yet Bishop Fell, in his memoir on the state of printing in the University of Oxford,* asserts, that that University possessed an exclusive right of transcribing and multiplying books by means of writing, which implies a species of Copyright.

Be this, however, as it may, our object is not to push our inquiry to so remote a period, but content ourselves with tracing from the time of the invention of printing, the first recognition of this right, and its subsequent allowance and confirmation; and we shall find, that as soon as it became valuable, it was claimed, and allowed; not only by favour of the sovereign, as in cases of privilege, or by consent among themselves, as in the by-laws of the Stationers' Company; but on principles of natural equity and justice. And though, in being minute, we may be thought tedious, we hope we shall not be considered as trifling; for the links that make up the chain of evidence, are sometimes of the slightest and most delicate texture.

It is the general opinion, that the art of printing was first brought into England by a mercer of London, of the name of Caxton, who had learned it at his own expense abroad: the first book printed by him in England being "The game and playe of the chesse," in the year 1474: § although there are not wanting some who claim for Oxford the honour of printing the first book; since a work has been discovered, entitled, "Exposicio sancti Jeronimi in simbolum apostolorum," which is expressed in the colophon to be printed at Oxford, 1468: "Jmpressa Oxonie Et finita Anno domini.

* Gutch's Collect. Curiosa. Vol I, p. 271.

§ This was the first book printed by him in England; but the first *English* book was printed three years before, "The Recuyell of the historyes of Troye, ——in the holy cyte of Colen," in 1471, by this same Caxton.

M.cccc.lxviij. xvij die decembris."* As this is, however, only a single instance, and the date may, perhaps, be a misprint, or designedly falsified; we may consider Caxton, in a practical point of view, as the first English printer.

Now Caxton, for the greater part of his printing career, being without competitors, needed no special protection for the works he published; and accordingly we do not find a single royal privilege granted for any of his works. And although Mr. Herbert appears to think he was appointed "King's printer," † yet it seems scarcely probable that this office would originate, when there was only a single printer,

* Connected with this book is a curious story, brought forward by Atkyns, in an action that he had as King's patentee against the Stationers' Company, for printing law books. He endeavoured to show by an M.S., said to have been in the Lambeth Library, that printing was first introduced into this country by Henry VI, who was moved thereto by Archbishop Bourchier; that this Oxford printer was brought over to England at the King's expense; and that the first printers were the King's sworn servants. From these facts he sought to derive a certain prerogative or perpetual copyright in the King, as being the first means of introducing printing into this country. Most even of those, however, who agree in thinking this book a proof of the earlier exercise of the art of printing in this country than can be adduced in favour of Caxton, and that it must have been executed by some foreigner, who found his way to England on the dispersion of the workmen of Guttenberg, Fust, and Schœffer, at the siege of Mentz; yet concur in the opinion, that as the pretended Lambeth M.S. has never been heard of since, so it never was anything but a forgery, designed solely to serve Atkyns's purposes.

† He says, "In M.S. at the beginning of a copy of Caxton's Chronicle, coeval with the publication, he is styled, 'Regius impressor.' This is further confirmed in the epilogue to 'Thymage, or myrrour of the world.'" Herb. Typ. Ant. p. 2.

The M.S. thus referred to, is in a copy of the work that belonged to Mr. Tutet, and is as follows: "Presens Liber pertinet ad Willm Purde emptus a Willmo Caxton, Regius Jmpressor vicesimo Nouembris Anno Regni Rēs Edwardi quarti vicesimo secundo." And the passage in the epilogue of "Thymage, or myrrour of the world," is "whiche book J began first to translate the second day of Janyuer the yer of our Lord, M.CCCC.lxxx. And fynysshed the viij day of Marche the same yere, And the xxj yere of the Regne of the most Crysten kyng. Kynge Edward the fourth. Vnder the shadowe of whos noble proteccion I haue emprysed and fynysshed this sayd lytyl werke and boke. Besechynge Almyghty god to be his protectour and defendour agayn alle his Enemyes," &c.

But when we consider the very full and minute account we have of upwards of as it could be of no value. But when several began to exercise the art of printing, it was then very natural that the king should select one out of the rest, the most expert, or the best recommended; especially to print papers of state and matters of government. And, accordingly, not long after, we find one William Faques, or Fakes, who styles himself "Regius impressor," in a proclamation against clipped money in 1504; † and from that time to the present, there has been a regular succession of persons holding that office.

The first instance that we have of an exclusive privilege for printing a book, occurs in the year 1518; and the occasion of it may be traced, not so much in the increase of printers by that time, as in the paucity of materials for the exercise of their trade; that is to say, the very few writings of immediate temporary interest which were then produced. It was printed by Richard Pynson, who succeeded Faques as "regius impressor;" and is entitled, "Oratio Richardi Pacei in Pace nuperrime composita," &c. Colophon: "Impressa Londini anno verbi incarnati M.D.XVIII. idibus Nouembris per Richardum Pynson regium impressorem *cum priuilegio* à rege indulto *ne quis hanc orationem intra biennium* in regno Angliæ *imprimat* aut alibi impressam et importatam in eodem regno Angliæ vendat." §

After this, privileges were, during the reign of Henry the Eighth, very freely granted. We find patents to several printers for seven years, for all books they may have then printed, or thereafter should print, to be computed from the date of the publication: as one to John Gowghe or Gough,

fifty productions of Caxton's press, and that never in any one of these, does he style himself "regius impressor;" although he often descends into the most minute details as to at whose cost and instigation he began to print his works, we can hardly think an M.S. note sufficient to establish the fact, contradicted as it is by his silence on the point. As to the extract from the Epilogue of "Thymage, or myrrour of the world," it is quite evident that, even as a collateral proof it is of little effect; and as a direct, is scarcely better than none at all.

† Herb. Typ. Ant. vol. i, p. 308. § Herb. Typ. Ant. vol. i. p. 264.

in 1540; to Thomas Berthelet, in 1538, "for sixe yeres"; and to Richard Banks, in 1540. There is also a patent to Reginald Wolfe, of the office of King's printer, in Latin, Greek, and Hebrew, with a prohibition to print such books as were therein specially assigned to him; or such books as "*propria sua industriâ, diligentiâ, atque labore conquisivit.*" *

Here we meet, for the first time, with a distinct acknowledgment of the existence of property in a literary work, wholly separate from the value of the materials employed in setting it before the public; a property 'acquired,' as we are told, 'by the patentee's own industry, diligence, and labour.' That these words refer to a mental outlay on the patentee's part, or on the part of another on account of the patentee, either in composing, abridging, or translating a work, is very evident, from the use of the word "conquisivit"—that the patentee "had acquired to himself:" how could the patentee have otherwise acquired more property in one book that he printed, than another; unless he had expended money, or mental labour in its composition? It, therefore, is a distinct proof of the recognition of literary property; and although we find it here in its infancy sheltered under the power of royal prerogative, we shall soon have to notice it as standing on firmer and surer grounds than the patronage of any prince—on the acknowledged justice and equity of its claim.

In the meantime had occurred, what may be considered as the first case of piracy of copyright on record.† Wynken de Worde had printed a Treatise on Grammar, by Robert Witinton, in 1523; which one Peter Trevers, or Treveris, had taken the liberty of re-printing; and Robert Witinton, in a subsequent edition, printed by De Worde in 1533, attacks

* Rym. Fœdera, vol. xv, p. 150.

† It was a common practice among the earlier printers, to join together in an impression of a work, and then print their own several title pages to the respective copies which they took. Thus we find many old books, purporting to be by different printers, and even of different years, and yet the body of the text is the same throughout. So that, although we may meet with works prior to the one cited in the text, which appear to have been printed by two or more printers

Trevers with great severity for this act. He indeed, seemingly lays the blame only on the incorrectness and faultiness of the edition; but it is clear, from Mr. Herbert's complete contradiction of such being the case,† that the chief crime in the eyes of the author and his publisher, was the *reprinting* the work at all. To prevent a recurrence of this, they procured a privilege from the king for the second edition.

About this time, also, we find a privilege for printing, which upon the face of it, though not in express words, is granted in consideration of the claims an author has to his copy. It is dated in 1530, and is in favour of "maistre Jehan Palsgraue Angloys natyf de Londres, et gradue de Paris," for a book to teach the French language, which he is said to have "made with a great and long continued dyligence;" and in which, "besydes his great labours, payns, and tyme there about employed, he hath also at his proper coste and charge put in prynt;" wherefore, continues the patent, "*we greatly moued and stered* by dewe consyderation of his sayd *long tyme and great dyligence* about this good and very necessary purpose employed, and also of his sayd *great costes and charges* bestowed about the imprintyng of the same, haue liberally and benignely graūnted vnto the sayd maister Palsgraue our fauorable letters of priuilege, concernynge his sayd boke, called, Lesclarcissement de la langue francoyse, for the space and terme of seuyn yeres next and immedyatly after the date hereof enswyng." &c.*

As printers improved, more books were published, and more privileges granted, as they were found to become more necessary. The following is a remonstrance contained in a letter from Grafton to Lord Cromwell, in August,

about the same time; yet the one alluded to above, is the first one we know for certainty to have been printed by one printer in opposition to another.

† Mr. Herbert even thought, that it was probable that Witinton might allude to some other edition printed by this Trevers; so little foundation did there appear to him to be for Witinton's bitter attack on this ground. Typ. Ant. vol. I, p. 187.

* Herb. Typ. Ant. vol. I, p. 470-1

1537,* respecting an apprehended attempt to reprint the bible, which he had just brought out, commonly known as "Matthew's Bible."

"And where as I wryt vnto yor lordship for a preuye seale to be a defence vnto the enemyes of this byble I vnderstonde that yor lordshipes mynde is that I shall not nede it. But now moost gracyous̄ lorde ffor as moche as this worke hath bene brought forthe to o^{r} moost & costly laboures & charges which charges amount aboue the some of £500 and I haue caused of these same to be prynted to the some of 1500 bookes complete, which now by reason that of many this worke is highly com̄ded, there are that will and dothe go about the pryntynge of the same worke agayne in a lesser letter, to the entent that they maye sell their lytle bookes better chepe then I can sell these gret, and so to make that I shall sell none at all, or elles very fewe, to the vtter vndoynge of me yor orato^{r} & of all those my credyto^{r}s that hath bene my comforters and helpers therin. And now this worke thus set forthe w^{t} great stodye & laboures shall soch p̄sons (moued w^{t} a lytle couetousnes to the vndoynge of other for their awne pryuate welthe) take as a thynge done to their handes, in which halffe the charges shall not come to them that hath done to yor poore orato^{r}. And yet shall they not do yt as they fynde yt, but falsefye the texte, that I dare saye, looke how many sentences as are in the byble, euen so many fautes & erroures shalbe made therin."——"Ye and to make yt more trewer then yt is, therfore douchemen dwellynge w^{t}in this realme go about the pryntynge of ytt wch can nether speke good englyshe, ner yet wryte none, and they wilbe both the prynters & correcto^{r}s therof, because of a lytle couetousnes that wyll not bestow xx or xl£ to a learned man to take payne in yt to haue yt well done. *It* were therfore (as yor Lordship dothe euydently perceaue) *a thynge vnreasonable to p̄myt* or soffer *them* (which now hath no soche busynes) *to enter into the laboures of them that hath*

* Cott. M.S, Cleop. E. v. p. 325.

had bothe sore trouble & vnreasonable charges. And the truthe is this that if yt be prynted by any other before these be solde (which I thynke shall not be this iii yere at the least, that then am I yor poore Orato^r vtterly vndone. Therfore by yor moost godly fauo^r if I maye obtayne the Kynges moost gracyous priuiledge that none shall prynt them tyll these be solde, which at the least shall not be this iii yere, yor lordship shall not fynde me vnthankfull, but that to the vttermost of my power I wyll consyder yt," &c.

Let us now consider how the foregoing facts operate in support of a right of literary property. It may be urged, that these very privileges, which have been dwelt on as in favour of Copyright, are so many proofs that no such a right was at that time thought to exist, except by virtue of the prerogative; for that no man would have cared to secure a right, as was here done by a royal privilege, had he known it to be valid in itself; but that, even putting this very obvious objection altogether aside, the privileges themselves contradict the very view they are brought to support; for all the instances above adduced, with the exception of one alone, are for a limited number of years, and how can instances of *limited* privileges be relied on as proofs of an *unlimited* right?

To these objections we reply, first, that in the infancy of this property, it was very natural for a man to have recourse to the readiest and most effectual way of securing it, which was by the protecting shadow of the king's privilege; for at that time the king's legal prerogative was the best title that could be relied on in the courts of common law. Besides, the king and his council regulated what books should be read and what not, and it was not safe to buy every publication; therefore the king's privilege further acted as a guarantee and protecting recommendation of the book.

And, secondly, we say, that a mistake is made as to the object with which these privileges are brought forward. They are adduced simply in favour of a broad principle, and not with a view to any particular application; and more stress is not laid on one for seven years, than on one for three. The principle recognized, namely, the protection of literary property, is all that is contended for: not the peculiar circumstances connected with it. Indeed it is most probable that the parties applying for these privileges, never looked beyond the protection of the one edition they printed; there was but one class of readers, an impression was calculated on which would supply their wants, and the only time for which a privilege was valuable, was, till it was sold off.* Second, third, and fourth editions, were not confidently looked to, with the calculating eyes of modern bibliopoles, as a means of repayment for their vast outlays at the commencement.

Therefore, the foregoing facts prove, that as soon as by the increase of printers, and the improvements in printing, it became possible for one man by printing another's copy, to avail himself of the money and labour expended by the other upon its production, without sharing in the cost, and so to undersell him; so soon was the injustice of such a proceeding on all sides proclaimed: that it was distinctly acknowledged, that by the rules of common justice and equity, a man was entitled to that which he had gained to himself either by mental labour, or by the expenditure of his money: and that this view was fully supported by the language in which the patents were couched; for, unlike other monopolies, there was no attempt to found the granting of them solely on the King's generosity; but, on the contrary, a statement was introduced of the reason for which they were conceded, namely—that the author had spent much time and labour in the composition of the work, or that the printer had laid out great sums of money, and these were the grounds on which the King was induced to grant them.

* See Grafton's Letter, ante p. 8. And if this was the case with works like the Bible, which might well be thought to afford a prospect of subsequent editions, how much more so must it have been in works of an ephemeral nature. It is evident that in these early stages of printing, the main expenses were in the mechanical part of the process, which are now transferred to the literary portion.

CHAPTER II.

FROM THE INCORPORATION OF THE STATIONER'S COMPANY IN 1556, TO THE REBELLION IN 1640.

SUCH was the state of literary property until the reign of Philip and Mary, when it being found, that 'many false fond books, and ballads, rhymes, and other lewd treatises in the English tongue, both heretical and seditious,' were being issued from the press; it was determined to unite the printers into one body, the heads of which should be responsible for the individual members; and the general conduct of which, could thus be more easily watched, and more effectually controuled. Letters patent were therefore passed, constituting the Stationer's Company, the 4th day of May, 1556. The Stationers, it would appear, were a Company before this date, but this was the commencement of their existence as a corporation. By their charter, they were allowed to make by-laws for the guidance of their members; and *no one but a member of their society,* was to be allowed to practise or exercise the art or mystery of printing within the dominions of England.*

This was a material step, although not an immediate one, to firmly securing the right of the first publisher to the exclusive printing of any work he might undertake; for the printers now having the power to make laws among themselves on the subject, could not fail soon to recognize the justice and expediency of such a provision. Accordingly,

* Luckombe's hist. of printing, p. 176.

we find them, within two or three years after the formation of their Company, requiring every one who printed a work to first enter it in their register-book, for which they paid a certain sum as for a license; and any one omitting to do so, or printing a *book belonging to another member*, was fined.*

Patents which till then had been for particular books, and were but a proper protection to the patentees in securing them the due fruits of their labour, began in the succeeding reign of Queen Elizabeth to be greatly abused. On one person was sometimes conferred an exclusive right to print all books of a particular class: thus, the right of printing all books of common-law was secured to one man; all A. B. C's. and Catechisms to another; all almanacs and prognostications to a third; all music-books to a fourth; besides patents of particular books to individuals who did not belong to the company, and were not printers, but farmed the right to such as were, at exorbitant sums.†

These monopolies pressed so hard upon the poorer sort of printers, that they petitioned the Queen against them; and this expedient meeting with little success, they, being driven by the desperate state of their circumstances, not only began to question the right of the Queen to grant them, but even proceeded to print works in defiance of the patents.

They did not, however, stop here, for emboldened by their present success, they began, says Strype, even to print books, *the copies whereof had been bought of the authors for their money*, or else given to those that had the property in them to make their benefit of. They set at defiance the power of their own Company; and although complaint was made to the Privy Council, and the matter being referred to commissioners, was settled for a time; yet it soon again broke out, and the Privy Council was again petitioned that these disorders might be put a stop to. Among other reasons urged,

* Register Book, *passim*.

† Strype, Herb. Typ. Ant., &c.

'No books at all,' it was said, 'would be printed within a short time. For commonly *the first printer was at charge for the author's pains,* and some other such like extraordinary cost; whereas any other that would print it after him, came to the copy gratis, and so he might sell cheaper, better than the first printer, and the first printer should never utter his books. Besides, the second printer might better the first impression by notes, tables, difference in paper, or volume, (as it is easier to amend than to first invent), which would also hinder the sale of the first printer's books to his utter undoing. These inconveniences seen, *every man would strain courtesy who should begin;* so far that in the end all printing would decay in the realm, to the utter undoing of the whole Company of Stationers.' *

That these irregularities and contempts of authority should have occurred, was not from want of ordinances and decrees on the subject; but from the liberty and license taken, owing to the troubles and jealousies that were fomented and kept alive in this reign, both by enemies at home and abroad, and which by fully occupying the attention of the government, prevented them from attending to matters wholly of a civil nature. For the Queen, directly on her coming to the throne, had issued injunctions† in which she positively prohibited any one from printing "any maner of booke or paper, of what sort, nature, or in what language soeuer it be, *except the same be first licenced* by her Maiestie, by expresse woordes in writing, or by six of her priuie Councell: or be perused & licenced by the Archbishops of Canterburie and Yorke, the Bishop of London, the Chauncelors of both Universities, the Bishop being Ordinarie, and the Archdeacon also of the place where any such shall be printed, or by two of them, whereof the Ordinarie of the place to be alwayes one;" on pain, "that the partie shall be punished by order

* Strype.

† "Injunctions given by the Queen's Maiestie. Anno domini. 1559." in Brit. Mus.

of the sayde Commissioners, as to the quality of the fault shall be thought meete."

Now as no book could be published without license, and as no license was given to print a work, which belonged to another by purchase or usage, the property in a copy would have been sufficiently protected by these injunctions, had they been strictly obeyed. But that they were far from being so, we find by a decree being issued by the Star Chamber in 1566,* for the reformation of divers disorders in printing, which was the first decree ever made by this Court respecting printing.

It enacted, 'that the printing any book against the force and meaning of any ordinance, prohibition, or commandment, contained or to be contained in any the statutes, or laws of the realm, or in any injunctions, letters patent, or ordinancies, past or set forth, or to be past or set forth, should be visited with the forfeiture of all such books, and disability to exercise the art of printing, besides imprisonment for three months without bail or mainprize.' And in order to keep the printers still more under control, they were enjoined to enter into 'their several recognisances of reasonable sums of money to her Majesty, with sureties or without, as the ecclesiastical commissioners should think expedient; truly to observe all the said ordinances, well and truly yield all such forfeitures, and in no point be resisting, but in all things aiding the said master and wardens of the said company and their deputies for the true execution of the premises.'

Notwithstanding this decree, we find afterwards complaints made against some who had given bonds, and yet broke through all regulations. Accordingly, in 1586, another decree was issued, † reciting that the former had been disregarded and broken through; by reason, it was supposed, that 'the

* Luck. Hist. of Print. p. 104. † Lansd. M.S. cod. 905.

pains and penalties contained and set down in the same had been too light and small for the correction and punishment of so grievous and heinous offences; and so the offenders and malefactors in that behalf had not been so severely punished as the qualities of their offences had deserved;' and therefore enacted, 'that no printers who had been admitted within the last six months, were to exercise their trade, until the excessive number of printers should be diminished.'

No printing was to be carried on elsewhere, than in the city of London; except one press at Oxford, and one also at Cambridge. And the directions as to licensing, contained in the Queen's injunctions of 1559, were here renewed under severe penalties.

But what more particularly distinguished this decree is an enactment in favor of Copyright, which perhaps was also included in the one of 1566. * For it is by this decree enacted, 'that no one shall print any book or other paper, contrary to any statute, letters patent, &c., or *contrary to any allowed ordinance* set down for the good government *of the Company of Stationers* within the city of London.' That these words alluded to the protection of the property in the copies is manifest from the recital of a proclamation in the subsequent reign, † which states, that whereas this last decree had been evaded, amongst other ways, "by printing beyond sea such allowed books, works, or writings, as had been imprinted within the realm by such to whom the sole printing thereof, by letters patent, or *lawful ordinance or authority* did appertain;" and therefore commands, that the same punishment shall be inflicted on persons importing, as on persons offending under that decree.

* I have not been able to meet with the decree of 1566, in any other than an abridged form; but as the clause in this decree of 1586 seems taken from the one of 1566, it is likely the same words would be found in the latter document if examined.

† 25th Sep. 1623.

The next decree we have to notice, is one in the 13th of Charles the First, § by which printers were placed under several arbitrary regulations, and the number of those allowed to keep a press, limited to twenty.

One of the redeeming features in this otherwise despotic act, was the protection it afforded Copyright, by the following clause, which enacted, 'that no one should import, or put to sale any books, which the Company of Stationers, or any other person had, or should by any letters patent, order, or *entrance in their register book or otherwise,* have the right, privilege, authority, or allowance solely to print; on penalty of forfeiture of books, and such fine as that Court should think fit.'

§ 11th July, 1637. Brit. Mus. M.S.

CHAPTER III.

FROM THE REBELLION IN 1640, TO THE RESTORATION IN 1660.

Nor was the protection thus justly afforded to Copyright under the legitimate government, wholly lost sight of amidst the troubles that shortly ensued. For although in the anarchy and confusion of order and property, which accompanied the rebellion, several attempts were made to procure that all works, without exception, should be open to any to print: yet Offspring, Teatly, Burges, Gouge, Byfield, Seaman, Calamy, and a number of other divines, who were on favorable terms with the party which then prevailed in Parliament, made strong representations against such a practice.

They urged, 'that to their knowledge, very considerable sums of money had been paid by stationers and printers to many authors, for the copies of such useful books as had been imprinted. In regard whereof,' they said, 'we conceive it to be both just and necessary, that they should enjoy a property for the sole imprinting of their copies. For unless they do, all scholars will be utterly deprived of any recompense from the stationers or printers, for their studies and labour in writing or preparing books for the press. Besides, if the books that are printed in England be suffered to be imported from beyond the seas, or in any other way re-imprinted, to the prejudice of those who bear the charges of the impressions, the authors and the buyers will be abused by vicious impressions, to the great discouragement of learned men, and extreme danger of all kinds of good learning.'

These and similar representations had so much weight with the House, that in an ordinance they afterwards published on the 14th of June, 1643,* 'for suppressing the late great abuses and disorders in printing,' reciting, amongst other things, that divers persons, "(*contrary to former orders and the constant custom* used among the Stationers' Company) had taken liberty to print, vend, and publish the most profitable vendible copies of books belonging to the Company and other Stationers;" they ordered, inter alia, that all books should be "entered in the register book of the Company of Stationers, *according to ancient custom;*" and that no one should print or import printed, "any book lawfully licensed and entered in the register book of the said Company, for any particular member thereof, *without the license and consent of the owner thereof;*" on pain of forfeiting the same to the owner, "and such further punishment as should be thought fit." Wardens, &c., empowered to make search, seize copies, and break presses, "employed in printing or reprinting books by such as have no lawful interest in them;" and to bring the compilers, printers, &c., before either of the Houses, "that so they might receive such further punishments as their offences should demerit."

This ordinance also contained enactments for the licensing of all books before publication; and when Milton, in his noble speech for the liberty of unlicensed printing, in the following year, attacked it with all the force of argument, the poignancy of satire, and the enthusiasm of a spirit-stirring appeal in favour of liberty; he at the same time carefully guarded against its being thought, that he objected to those parts of it, which related "to the just retaining of each man his several copy; which God forbid," he exclaims, "should be gainsaid."

* Scobell's Acts and Ord. of Parlmt. pp. 44, 5. ed. 1658.

In another ordinance of the Usurpation Parliament, passed the 20th of September, 1649,* for putting down false and scandalous pamphlets, and regulating printing, and restraining it "from too arbitrary and general an exercise," the following enactment was made:—

That any person *printing* or reprinting any books entered in the registry book of the Stationers' Company, *without the consent of the owner* thereof, or stitching or binding the same, should forfeit all such books, and 6s. 8d. for each.

* Scobell's Acts and Ord.

CHAPTER IV.

FROM THE RESTORATION IN 1660, TO THE ACCESSION OF WILLIAM AND MARY, 1688.

As the liberty of the press had met with but little sympathy even from the loudest declaimers for freedom, so it could not be expected to receive much consideration at the hands of the restored government, who could trace in it one of the great means of their original expulsion. But as there was no Star-Chamber any longer, to give an appearance of legality to the mandates of the Court, application was obliged to be made to Parliament to legislate on that subject; and that compliant body hesitated not to reforge for the press its old fetters. To enter into this, however, would be beside our subject at present, which is merely to show the authority that the act that they passed* gave to the right of copy in the owner, by the following clause :—

In which it is enacted, that no one should print any book or books, "which any person or persons, by force or virtue of any letters patent granted or assigned, or which should hereafter be granted or assigned to him or them, or (where the same are not granted by any letters patent), *by force or virtue of any entry* or entries thereof duly made or to be made in the register book of the said Company of Stationers, or in the register book of either of the Universities respectively, had or should have the right, privilege, authority, or allowance, solely to print, *without the consent of the owner or owners of such book* or books;" nor should bind, stitch, &c., on pain of forfeiting

* 13 & 14 Car. II. c. 33.

the same, and 6s. 8d. for each book, and being proceeded against as an offender against that act.

And by another clause, it obliged the printer of every work to reserve three copies; one for the King's library, and one for each of the Universities of Oxford and Cambridge.*

The entry of works in the register book of the Stationers' Company, had been so often recognised and treated as equivalent to proof of ownership by decrees and other acts, that a legal title was thought to be attained by it, even paramount to that of the king's patentee, if he had not registered his work; and Atkyns, who held a patent from the king for printing all books touching the common law, finding parties acting in defiance of it, on the pretext of priority of title by entry, petitioned the king, who issued a proclamation,† wherein, after stating that differences had arisen between the Stationers' Company and Mr. Atkyns, to whom the king had granted the sole right of printing all law books, *owing to divers copies* of such books *being entered* in the register books of the Stationers' Company, by which *a private property* was pretended to be *gained* thereto; it was stated to be his Majesty's pleasure, that no book concerning the common law should be entered in the register book, so as to give the person entering it any property in such book, but that the printing thereof be solely reserved to the said Edward Atkins.

A cause, in which this point was involved, was at this time pending in the Court of Common Pleas, and is the first case on record concerning Copyright before a legal tribunal. It is not regularly reported, but was quoted in the case of the Company of Stationers *v.* Parker, 1 Jac. II., Skinner's

* This was the first foundation of the present claim of public bodies to copies of every work published. Sir Thomas Bodley, had, as far back as 1610, made an agreement with the Stationers' Company, by which they agreed to give a copy of every work printed in the Company to the University of Oxford; but this was a matter of private agreement, and not a compulsory clause of a statute.

† Dated the 8th of Nov. 1671.

Rep. p. 234. The circumstances were these: 'Roper, the plaintiff, had bought of the executors of Mr. Justice Crook, the third part of his reports; Streater, the defendant, had a grant from the King, and printed upon Roper; upon which the latter brought an action of debt upon the stat. 14 Car. II. Streater pleaded the King's grant, upon which Roper demurred, and judgment was given for the plaintiff.' *

And although this judgment was reversed afterwards in Parliament, yet its authority was not shaken, since the reversal proceeded upon the grounds that the *copy belonged* to the King. Besides, the Judges were not consulted on the occasion, and it is not clear that they would have supported the reversal; for although the majority of the Lords concurred in reversing the judgment, it was not till after long debate and consultation; and the opinions of the Judges were not taken; for when the question was put, 'that the Judges be heard in this case,' it was carried in the negative, 'dissentiente Anglesey.'

* Roper *v.* Streater, M. T. 24 Car. II., Rot. 237. It was said afterwards, in the case of the Stationers' Company *v.* Parker, Skin. 233, in reference to the above case, and in answer to the argument of there being no right of copy at common law decided in this case, since it was brought on the Statute of 14 Car.II. that 'although it was true, that the action was brought on the act of 14 Car. II., yet that Statute did not give a *right*, but only an *action of debt;*' therefore, that the case was a precedent of an action on the common-law right of the owner.

Perhaps this case of Roper *v.* Streater was the one alluded to by Sergeant Pemberton in T. T. 29 Car. II., 1 Mod. Rep. 256, Stationers' Company *v.* Seymour, where he says, "When Sir Orlando Bridgeman was Chief Justice in this court, there was a question raised concerning the validity of a grant of the sole printing of any particular book, with a prohibition to all others to print the same, how far it should stand good against them that claim a property to the copy, paramount to the king's grant; and opinions were divided on the point." If so, the learned sergeant states the case rather differently when he says, "that opinions were divided on the point." Perhaps he refers to the case before it was decided, whilst it was pending in the court; and this appears more probable, since Sir Orlando Bridgeman was not Chief Justice, when judgment was pronounced, having been then recently elevated to the dignity of Lord Keeper.

The act of Charles the Second above mentioned, was at first made only for a limited period, but was afterwards renewed from time to time till the end of the session, 31 Car. II., which was in May, 1679, when it was suffered to expire. The many debates about the Popish Plot, the bill for excluding the Duke of York from the throne, the impeachment of the Lord Treasurer Danby, the ill-humour of the Parliament, and their encroaching spirit, the short period of their session, their hasty prorogation and subsequent dissolution, are all reasons why this bill was not again renewed, as it most likely would have been under other circumstances. And the two subsequent Parliaments which were held in this reign, were conducted so tumultuously, betrayed such a spirit of faction, and were dissolved so hastily, that no time was found for discussing a bill like the present one, so comparatively unimportant at that moment.

As soon as the legislative protection was thus removed from the copies of works, the meaner and least honourable men of the Stationer's Company, who had little to lose, having no copies of their own, and much to gain by pirating the valuable works of their wealthier neighbours, and so reaping without cost what it had cost others much to sow, began without shame or fear to appropriate to themselves the labours and property of others; whereupon the principal stationers met together in council, on the 17th of August, 1681, to take some effectual steps to prevent a practice so ruinous to the best interests of their trade, and agreed upon the following by-law, which was accordingly passed.*

It recited, that 'Whereas several members of the company had great part of their estate in copies, and by ancient usage of the company, when any book or copy was duly entered in the register book of the company, such person to whom such entry is made, was, and always had been, reputed and

* Register Book.

taken to be the proprietor of such book or copy, and ought to have the sole printing thereof, which privilege and interest was then of late often violated and abused;' and ordained, that where any such entry was duly made, any other person printing, or importing, selling, binding, or stitching the same, without the consent of the owner or his assigns, should forfeit 12d. for every such copy so printed or imported.*

As our present object is confined strictly to tracing the different steps by which the Law of Copyright arrived at its present state, we pass by, as foreign to our purpose, the legal arguments and discussions that now arose in several cases, as to the King's power of granting exclusive patents for different works; since they were not so much cases interfering with the particular Copyright of individuals, as restrictions on the general liberty of printing.

On the accession of James II. the 13 and 14 Car. II. c. 33, was revived by the 1st of Jac. II., c. 17, for the term of seven years, and thence to the end of the next Session of Parliament.

* This was afterwards, on the 7th of October, approved of and confirmed by the Lord Chancellor and the Lords Chief Justices, to whom it was submitted for that purpose, pursuant to a statute passed in the 19 of Henry VII. which requires that all by-laws made by companies, shall be first examined and approved of by the persons therein named, under penalty of £40 for every default.

CHAPTER V.

FROM THE REVOLUTION IN 1688, TO THE ACCESSION OF ANNE.

In William and Mary's reign, when this act, commonly called 'The 'Licensing Act,' was about to expire, it was renewed by the 4 W. & M. c. 24, sec. 15, for a year from the 13th day of Feb. 1692, O.S. and from thence until the end of the next Session of Parliament.

It may appear curious that in times when liberty was so zealously asserting her rights, a bill that thus completely fettered the press should have been again renewed; but it was in a manner secretly passed through the House of Commons, it being an amendment proposed in committee to a general act for renewing about a dozen of statutes then about to expire; and when the motion was put that the house agreed with the committee in that amendment, it was only carried by a majority of 19 out of 179 members present. On the bill being submitted to a Committee in the House of Lords, the house, after reading the petition of several booksellers and bookbinders, and others, dealers in books and printing, praying to be heard before the passing of the bill, ordered that they should be heard. But they do not appear to have met with much success, as the bill was soon after read a third time; on which occasion two riders were offered, but these being negatived the bill was passed. A protest was, however, drawn up and signed by eleven Lords, which thus concludes their reasons against the bill,—

"Because it subjects all learning and true information to the arbitrary will and pleasure of a mercenary, and perhaps ignorant, licenser; *destroys the property of authors in their copies;* and sets up many monopolies."*

We learn from 'Reasons humbly offered to be considered before the act for printing be renewed,'† that this 'destruction of property' referred to certain mal-practices in the management of the register book of the Company of Stationers. The Company, it appears, not being compelled to do so by any express words in the statute, sometimes asked large sums for making an entry, and at others refused or neglected to enter books; and not unfrequently made false entries and erasures to the confusion of all property. It was also alleged, that the terms of the Act itself were liable to misconstruction, as it seemed to make the fact of an entry equivalent to proof of legal ownership. "By the said Act it is enacted, that a book being licensed and entered into the Register-book of the Company of Stationers, it is forbid to be printed without the owner's licence (who by virtue of that entry is owner) under the penalty of 6s. 8d. per book; which Register hath (by the undue practices of the Master and Wardens), been so ill kept, that many entries have been unduly made, insomuch that the true proprietors, both by purchase, licence, and entry, all duly made of several books, which afterwards have been erased, or the leaves wherein they have been written have been cut out, and undue entries made to others who had no right, which is directly contrary to the plain words and meaning of the said Act, whereby the owners have not only been defrauded of their right, but also rendered liable to the penalty of 6s. 8d. per book for all the books they printed, sold or bound. Many learned authors have been defrauded of their rights thereby, who, after many years' pains and study, and after-

* Lords' Journals.

† In the Brit. Mus., a printed sheet.

wards by a bare delivery of their books to be licensed, have been barred by surreptitious entries made in the said Register, (to instance, in the book called 'Regula Placitandi,' among many others, written by a learned lawyer and worthy Member of Parliament.)"

The Act so renewed was only of short duration, and another attempt was soon required to be made, to get its enactments again prolonged. Accordingly, on the 10th of February, 1694, O.S., when the Committee, appointed to inquire into what laws were expiring, or had expired, gave in their report, they recommended, amongst other laws, that the 13 and 14 Car. II., c. 33, should be revived. But the House rejected this recommendation, at the same time, however, ordering a Committee to be appointed to prepare and bring in a Bill, 'For the better Regulating of Printing and Printing Presses.'

A Bill was accordingly prepared and brought into the House on the 2nd of March, read a first time on the 7th, a second time on the 30th, and sent into Committee. On the latter day, a Petition was presented from the Master, Wardens, and Commonalty of the Company of Stationers, setting forth that they heard a Bill was depending in the House for the better regulation of Printing and Printing-Presses, and that if their property should not be provided for by the said Bill, not only the petitioners, but many widows and others, whose whole livelihood depended on the petitioners' property, would be utterly ruined.* They therefore prayed to be heard by counsel touching the said Bill.

What became afterwards of this Bill, we cannot learn; whether it was lost in the committee, or whether the report of the committee was never given in, on account of more pressing business, or the near termination of the session which occurred on the 3d of May. Perhaps it was a mea-

* House of Commons' Journals.

sure that satisfied neither party, for it appears probable that it was only brought forward to show that while the Commons refused to revive the Licensing Act, they were not unwilling to pass some measure of a more moderate nature to regulate the liberty of printing. We are, however, left to conjecture, for there were no debates on the subject, nor any information beyond what may be gleaned from the scanty details in the Commons' Journals.*

In the meantime the bill to continue the acts about to expire, was passed in the House of Commons, carried up to the Lords, and there on the 3rd of April committed; when, amongst other amendments to the bill, the very resolution which the Commons had rejected, of reviving the 13 and 14 Car. II, c. 33, was proposed and carried, and the bill, with this alteration, passed and sent down to the Commons for their concurrence. The Commons then desired a conference, which being had on the 18th of April, they submitted to their Lordships a great many reasons for not consenting to the renewal of that act. Amongst the rest: "Because that act prohibits printing any thing before entry thereof in the register of the Company of Stationers (except proclamations, acts of parliament, and such books as shall be appointed under the sign manual, or under the hand of a principal secretary of state); whereby both houses of parliament are disabled to order any thing to be printed; and the said Company are empowered to hinder the printing all innocent and useful books; and have an opportunity to enter a title to themselves and their friends, for *what belongs to and is the labour and right of others*." † The Lords then retired

* The last that was heard of this Bill, was on the 3rd of April, when the House ordered, that the Committee to whom the Bill was committed, should have power to send for persons, papers, and records.

† And another reason was, "Because that Act prohibits any one, not only to print books whereof another has entered a claim of property in the register of the Company of Stationers; but to bind, stitch, or put them to sale, and that

to their own house, and on the question being put, whether they agreed with the Commons in leaving out the clause, reviving the 13 and 14 Car. II, c. 33, it was resolved in the affirmative.

So that this act, commonly called the 'Licensing Act,' finally expired on the 25th of April, 1694; which was the end of the next session, after the expiration of a year from the 13th of February, 1692, O.S.

The same inconveniences arising as did on the former occasion, on the expiration of this act, the stationers soon afterwards convened a common-hall,* and passed a by-law, similar to the one of August, 1681. It recited: "Whereas divers members of this company have great parts of their estates in copies, duly entered in the register book of this company, which, by the ancient usage of the company, is, are, or always hath and have been used, reputed, and taken to be the right and property of such person and persons (members of this company), for whom or whose benefit such copy and copies are so duly entered in the register book of this company, and constantly bargained and sold, amongst the members of this company, as their property; and devised to children and others, for legacies, and to their widows for maintenance; and that he and they, to whom such copy and copies are so duly entered, purchased, or devised, ought to have the sole printing thereof:" And ordained, "for the better preservation of the said ancient usage from being invaded by evil-minded men, and to prevent the abuse of trade by violating the same," that 'where any such entry of a book was duly made, any one printing, importing, selling, binding, stitching, or exposing the same to sale, should forfeit the sum of 12d. for each copy, or part of such copy.'

under a great pecuniary penalty; though it is impossible for a bookbinder, stitcher, or seller, to know whether the book brought to him were printed by the proprietor or another."

* 14th May, 1694.

CHAPTER VI.

FROM THE ACCESSION OF ANNE, TO THE PASSING THE 8TH ANNE, C. 19.

BUT as the foregoing by-law did not have the desired effect, and some of the poorer sort of the printers, and others not belonging to the company, persisted in printing other men's copies: the parties aggrieved petitioned parliament in the years 1703, 1706, and again in 1709, to put a stop to these mal-practices, and to enact penalties against the offenders.

Some time before, in one of the petitions offered against the renewal of the licensing act, we find the following, suggested by the petitioners, as heads of a bill, they were willing to have passed. '1, That it should be made felony for any printer to neglect to put his name and address to any book he printed. 2, That a penalty should be fixed on seditious, treasonable, and scandalous books. 3, That "the proprietor should be *secured* in his particular copies, by giving him a *method of process*, and treble costs and damages against the invader." 4, That the register-book of the Company of Stationers should be duly rectified, and all fraudulent and false entries, and entries of popish books, and other illegal and scandalous books there entered, be expunged, and the true proprietor thus reinstated in his right.'

It is in fact the burden of almost all the petitions that we meet with, prior to the 8th of Anne, that *security* be given to the proprietor for *quiet enjoyment* of his property in his copies; not that a *property* in his copies be given to him.

It is his undoubted right, they say. In the petition above alluded to they assert: "The property of English authors hath been always *owned as sacred* among the traders, and generally forborne, hitherto to be invaded: but if any should invade such properties, *there is remedy*, by laws already made, and no other were ever thought needful till 1662."

Again, in another petition entitled "Reasons against the Act for Licensing," they say: "As for securing property, *it's secured by law already*, as our own experience may show; and before 1662, there was no Act of Parliament for regulating printing; it is the enclosed common that is intended by the patentees to be made a property by Act of Parliament. That particular property may be secured, is earnestly desired."

But although there was remedy, it was not equally clear what that remedy was. Copyright had been so long protected in the manner we have shown, by decrees and acts, that any other mode of proceeding was almost unknown.* Besides, what use was there in running the hazard of an action at law against persons, who could not, even in the event of success, pay the costs, much less the damages, that might be adjudged against them?

It was these circumstances that induced the respectable portion of the trade to earnestly desire that some step should be taken in Parliament to more effectually secure their property; and by the authority of the legislature, to proclaim, that their rights were no longer to be trampled on with impunity.

"They set forth to the Parliament," says Mr. Strype, in his edition of Stow's Survey of London, "that when the

* It is true, there was the instance in Charles the Second's time, soon after the expiration of the Licensing Act, in the King's Bench, of an action on the case, brought for printing the Pilgrim's Progress, 'of which the plaintiff was and is the true proprietor; whereby he lost the benefit and profit of his copy.' Poynder *v.* Bradyl, H. T. 31. Car. II. Lilly's Entries, p. 67. But this was a solitary case, and as it does not appear that the action was proceeded in, it could hardly operate as a precedent.

author had conveyed over his copy to any of them, they had a just and legal property thereunto. And that they had given sums of money for copies, and had settled those copies on their wives at marriage, or on their children at their deaths. And that at this time many widows and orphans had none other subsistence; and that the copies then in use had cost the present possessors (exclusively of all other charges of print and paper) at least £50,000. Urging further that this property was the same with houses and other estates, being agreeable to common law and good reason. To which might be added, that unless this liberty of printing upon the owners of copies were stopped, it would prove a great discouragement to the printing of many good books, offered by authors to the booksellers, who would not care to meddle in such uncertain gain, and thereby might ensue great prejudice to knowledge and learning."

And in another case given to the members in support of their application for a bill, the last reason or paragraph is as follows:—"The liberty now set on foot of breaking through this ancient and reasonable usage is no way to be effectually restrained, but by an Act of Parliament. For, *by common law, a bookseller can recover no more costs than he can prove damage;* but it is impossible for him to prove the tenth, nay perhaps the hundredth part of the damage he suffers, because a thousand counterfeit copies may be dispersed into as many different hands all over the kingdom, and he is not able to prove the sale of ten. Besides, the defendant is always a pauper; and so the plaintiff must lose his costs of suit. *No man of substance had been known to offend in this particular;* nor will any ever appear in it. Therefore, *the only remedy by the common law* is to confine a beggar to the rules of the King's Bench or Fleet; and there he will continue the evil practice with impunity. We therefore pray that *confiscation of counterfeit copies be one of the penalties* to be inflicted on offenders."

By which we may learn that the reason of applying for some law on the subject, was not because an author was thought to have no right in his copy, or no remedy for its infringement; but because it was sought to render his right more beneficial, by the remedy being made more effective. The action on the case could only give the damages arising from each particular sale of a copy proved at the trial; and the judgment obtained could have no effect on the pirated copies still remaining in the printer's hands, which he was still at the same liberty to attempt to dispose of as at first. Besides, the action on the case was a peculiarly inappropriate and expensive remedy against parties, who had no property to answer the event of the trial, and where the plaintiff, even when successful, was left to pay his own costs; for at this time no man of respectability or substance as has been already stated, had been known to offend in such a case.

In compliance, therefore, with the above petitions, leave was given to bring in a bill, which, we are told, went to the Committee as "A Bill to secure the undoubted property of copies for ever."* And as this Bill has had a very material effect on the property of authors, and has been adjudged to take away from them any common law right they before possessed, it will not be unprofitable to mark the steps by which it passed into a law.

On the 11th of January, 1709, O. S., say the Journals of the House of Commons, "Mr. Wortley† according to order presented to the House, 'A Bill for the encouragement of Learning, and for *securing* the property of copies of Books to the *rightful* owners thereof;' and the same was received and read a first time."

An early day was named for the second reading; but it

* Mr. Justice Willes, in Millar *v.* Taylor, 4 Burrow's Rep. p. 2333. But what authority the learned Judge had for this statement, does not appear.

† Afterwards the husband of the beautiful and accomplished Mary Pierrepoint, better known as Lady Mary Wortley Montague.

was suffered to pass by without any notice being taken till the 2nd of February, when was presented, "A Petition of the poor distressed printers and bookbinders, in behalf of themselves and the rest of the same trades, in and about the cities of London and Westminster; setting forth that the petitioners, who are in number at least five thousand, having served seven years' apprenticeship, hoped to have gotten a comfortable livelihood by their trades; but that the liberty lately taken, of some few persons printing books, to which they have no right to the copies, is such a discouragement to the bookselling trade, that no person can proceed to print any book without considerable loss, and consequently the petitioners cannot be employed, by which means the petitioners are reduced to very great poverty and want. And, praying that their deplorable case may be effectually redressed, in such a manner as to the house shall seem meet." The House ordered the petition to lie on the table, till the Bill before the House was read a second time, which it accordingly was on the 9th of the same month.

After several amendments had been made in Committee, it was read a third time on the 14th of March, and passed. The title was then fixed as, "An Act for the encouragement of learning, by *vesting* the copies of printed books in the authors, or purchasers of such copies, *during the times therein mentioned.*"

The Lords made some amendments, amongst the rest, the giving the further term of fourteen years in the event of the author surviving the first fourteen years; and the Commons having agreed to all of them except one, which was striking out the clause regulating the price of books, and which was subsequently abandoned by the Lords, the Bill was passed, and received the royal assent the same day, being the last of the session.

This act stands in the Statute Book as the 8 Annæ, c. 19. It recites that, "Whereas printers, booksellers, and other persons, have of late frequently taken the liberty of printing, reprinting, and publishing, or causing to be printed, reprinted, and published, books and other writings, without the consent of the authors or proprietors of such books and writings, to their very great detriment, and too often to the ruin of them and their families:" And enacts, "for preventing, therefore, such practices for the future, and for the encouragement of learned men to compose and write useful books;" that the author or his assigns of any book published before the 10th of April, 1710, should have the sole right of printing and publishing it, for the term of twenty one years, to commence from that day; and the author or his assigns of any book thereafter to be published, should have the sole right of printing and publishing for the term of fourteen years, from the date of publication; with a provision for a further term of fourteen years, if the author should be living at the expiration of the first. And any one printing such book within the period specified, without the owner's consent, should forfeit all such books or parts thereof, and 1d. for every sheet of the same, one half of the penalty to go to her Majesty, and the other to any one suing for the same.

The forfeiture and penalties were not to extend to cases where the title of a work had not been duly entered in the register book of the Stationers' Company, which entry the clerk of the Company was required to make, on payment of a fee of 6d.; and, on refusal, notice in the Gazette to be of like avail.

When books were sold at unreasonable prices, the Lord Archbishop of Canterbury, the Lord Chancellor, the Lord Keeper of the Great Seal, the Lord Bishop of London, the Lord Chief Justices of Queen's Bench, Common Pleas, the Lord Chief Baron of the Exchequer, the Vice Chancellors of the two Universities, or any one of them, on complaint being made, might inquire into the same, and regulate the price;

and any bookseller selling contrary to that regulation should forfeit £5 for every book so sold. *

Nine copies of each book were to be sent to the public libraries therein named, on penalty of £5, and the value of such copy. †

Nothing in the act was to extend to the prohibiting the importing or selling any books in Greek, Latin, or any other foreign language, printed beyond the seas.

All actions were to be brought within three months.

These were the principal provisions of this Bill, which concluded with this very general proviso: "That nothing in this act contained should extend, or be construed to extend, either to prejudice or confirm any right that the said Universities, or any of them, or any person or persons have or claim to have to the printing or reprinting any book or copy already printed or hereafter to be printed."

We have no account of any debates on the subject; nor indeed do we know what were the provisions of this Bill, as it was first introduced into the House of Commons: but we may fairly assume from the language of the petitions, and from the original title of the Bill, that it was submitted to the House, as a Bill to protect the property in Copyright of an author in perpetuity; and that the House, unwilling to run the hazard of such prospective legislation, as the enact-

* This clause was repealed by 12 Geo. II. c. 36.

† With regard to this clause it may be curious to observe the changes it went through, before it became as it now stands.

As the Bill was originally brought into the House of Commons, it was only for three copies to be delivered to the same public bodies, who were entitled to them, under the 13 & 14 Car. II. c. 33. In the passage of the Bill through the Commons, two more copies were added for the Edinburgh University and Sion College; and the Scotch Peers, in the House of Lords, not to be behind hand in letting so good an opportunity pass for enriching their public libraries, at the expense of the poor author, added accordingly four more copies for Scotland, making the nine in all.

ment of penalties and forfeitures for ever, took a middle course, and granting the penalties and forfeiture for a term, introduced a proviso, saving all rights an author might have by common law for a longer period, the same as if the act had never been made. It has been said that the proviso was only meant to save the rights of patentees; but, as has been well observed, if so, it was of no utility; since there is nothing in the act that could have extended to injure or confirm patent rights, they not being mentioned or comprised in any words therein. Besides, it is evident that the common-law right of an author was admitted at the time; not only by the proofs before adduced, but by the very language of the recital,—'that divers persons had taken the liberty of late,'—'for preventing therefore such practices for the future'—by which phrases, the legislature would never have denominated the exercise of what, till then, was a legal right; and the common-law right of an author being admitted, it could not with any reason be supposed to have been bartered away for so short a period as that of fourteen years, with the contingency only of a further term on the expiration of the first; and the books to be limited, even during that time, to what price, certain persons, named by the act, should consider as reasonable. But we shall have to return to this subject further on, in the famous case of Millar *v.* Taylor, and therefore shall not insist more on it in this place.

CHAPTER VII.

FROM THE PASSING THE 8 ANNE, C. 19, TO THE CASE OF MILLAR AGAINST TAYLOR, IN 1769.

A LONG period had not elapsed, before application was made to Parliament to amend the foregoing act. It would appear that most of the popular works, which appeared about this time, were reprinted in Ireland and in Holland, and imported into England, where, by reason of their cheapness, they met with a ready and scarcely concealed sale. For the penalty, by the 8 Annæ, c. 19, being only a penny per sheet and the forfeiture of the book, was not of a nature to deter those who were concerned in this profitable traffic; so that Parliament was applied to for further protection: and on a committee being appointed, pirated editions, printed abroad, of no less than twenty-nine different English authors, were placed before them. In pursuance of their recommendation, leave was then given to bring in a Bill 'to *make more effectual* the 8 of Anne, c. 19.'*

What the exact nature of this Bill was, or what were the amendments made to it in the Commons, we cannot ascertain; but its provisions seem to have undergone considerable change in their progress through the House, if we may infer anything from the alteration in its title, which was ordered to be "An Act for the better encouragement of learning, and the more effectual securing of the copies of printed books to the authors or purchasers of such copies during the times

* On the 12th of March, 1735.

therein mentioned, and for *repealing* an Act passed, &c., intituled, &c." (the 8 of Anne, c. 19.) It passed the Commons; but the second reading in the Lords was put off from day to day till the 19th of May, before which day the Parliament was prorogued.

On the 11th of February, 1737, this Bill was again brought forward in the House of Commons, and a division took place on the question that the Bill do pass, which was carried by a majority of 63, out of 237 members present. In the House of Lords it advanced a further stage than in the last session, for it passed a second reading, but was afterwards put off, for a month, on the question of the House going into committee on the 10th of May.

Finding that the opposition was too strong to this Bill to give any hopes of its being finally carried, its framers turned their attention more immediately to the remedy of the evils of foreign importation, and obtained leave on the 17th of April, in the following year, to bring in "A Bill for prohibiting the importation of books, reprinted abroad, which were originally printed in Great Britain." The words "and for limiting the price of books," were added to its title in its progress through the house. This Bill, like the foregoing, was thrown out in the House of Lords, although it reached as far as the motion for the third reading.

Such uninterrupted ill-success did not however prevent its promoters from bringing it forward again, at the next session of Parliament, and they reaped the usual reward of perseverance; for although an attempt was made to throw it out in the House of Lords, on the question of going into Committee, it was defeated, and the Bill finally passed on the 9th of May 1739, and received the royal assent on the 14th of June.* Perhaps their ultimate success was owing to the changed nature of the Bill; for it now contained only two

* 12 Geo. II. c. 36.

clauses; one, which so far from limiting the prices of books, expressly repeals the section of the 8 Anne c. 19, to that effect; and the other, which forbids the importation from abroad of any book first printed here within twenty years, on penalty of forfeiture of books, £5, and double the value of each copy so imported or knowing sold.†

Although the foregoing act prevented in a great measure the importation of pirated editions from Ireland, it did not prevent their being printed there: and to how great an extent this system of reprinting was carried, may be seen by the following extracts from a statement made by Richardson, the printer of Sir Charles Grandison, in 1753. It appears that some Irish printers, notwithstanding the extraordinary precautions he had taken, contrived to get proof sheets as the work was in the press, from some of his servants, and announced it for publication in Dublin, almost contemporaneously with the London edition.

He says: "It has been customary for the Irish booksellers to make a scramble among themselves who should first entitle himself to the reprinting of a new English book, and happy was he who could get his agent in England to send him a copy of a supposed saleable piece, as soon as it was printed and ready to be published. This kind of property was never contested with them by authors in England; and was agreed among themselves (*i. e.* among the Irish booksellers and printers,) to be a sufficient title, though now and then a shark was found, who preyed on his own kind, as the newspapers of Dublin have testified. But the present case will show to what a height of baseness such an undisputed licence is arrived." And he concludes his remonstrance with these observations: "After all, if there is no law to right the editor

† This Act was only temporary; but was continued by the 27 Geo. 2. c. 18, 33 Geo. 2. c. 16, and the 29 Geo. 3. c. 55. It is now expired, and the existing regulation against importation of books is 41 Geo. 3, c. 107. sec. 7.

and proprietor of this new work (new in every sense of the word), he must acquiesce; but with this hope, that, from so flagrant an attempt, a law may one day be thought necessary, in order to secure to authors the benefits of their own labours. At present the English writers may be said, from the attempts and practices of the Irish booksellers and printers, to live in an age of *liberty*, but not of *property*."

CHAPTER VIII.

THE CASE OF MILLAR AGAINST TAYLOR.

We now come to the famous copyright case of Millar *v.* Taylor, in the King's Bench in 1769; in which the nature, custom, and law of literary property were most fully and ably discussed.

The term given in old copies by the 8 Anne, c. 19, was twenty-one years, from the 10th of April, 1710; and therefore the earliest period in which the common-law right of the author in them, could come in question, was after the 10th of April, 1731. And we find that in 1735, and afterwards, injunctions were granted by the Court of Chancery restraining the printing of particular books, the copyright by statute in which had expired; and these were acquiesced under. But a doubt afterwards arising, a common law action, Tonson against Collins, was by consent brought to decide the right. The Court heard two arguments upon the case, but being then informed that the action was brought by collusion, and that the defendant would acquiesce in the judgment, which was to be used against third parties, refused to proceed with it, although the counsel for the defendant, we are told, argued the case *bonâ fide* and very ably.

Whilst this cause was pending in the common-law courts, several injunctions were refused in Chancery on that ground. As soon, however, as the reason was known why the Court would not proceed with the case of Tonson *v.* Collins, and that the leaning of the opinion of the Court, as far as it could be ascertained, was in favor of the plaintiff; the action was commenced of Millar against Taylor, which we are now about to notice. It must not be expected that we can give all the arguments, or objections, started on either side in this cause, since the judgments delivered by the Court occupy 97 pages of close 8vo. print.* All that we can hope to do, is to give a leading outline of the principles on which the case was argued, referring the more curious reader to the report itself for fuller information.

The facts were these: — Millar, a bookseller, purchased in 1729, from Thomson, the Copyright of his 'Seasons,' which had been published about a year before. In 1763, Taylor, the defendant, published an edition; and Millar accordingly brought the present action on the case for damages against him, on the supposed common-law right—since any right by statute had expired in 1756 or 7.

Reversing the order used at the trial, we shall commence first with the arguments adduced against literary property, and afterwards proceed to confute them.

And against the right of literary property, the arguments were divided into three heads.

First, That by its very nature no such property could exist.

Secondly, That if it could eixst, yet there was no proof that it did exist.

And thirdly, that if there was proof that such a property did once exist, yet the stat. 8 of Anne, c. 19, had taken it away; and on principles of public policy it ought not to be again revived.

And first, that by the very nature of literary productions, no property in them could exist. For to claim a property in a thing, it was said, it is necessary that it should have certain qualities; it should be of a *corporeal substance*, be *capable of occupancy or possession*, it should have *distinguishable proprietary marks*, and be a subject of *sole and exclusive*

* Burrow's Rep. Vol. IV. p. 2310-2407.

enjoyment. But the property claimed, possessed none of these indispensable characteristics. It had no *corporeal substance:* for the claim was not made to the print and paper; but to the ideas contained in a book, which are intangible and incorporeal. It was not *capable of occupancy or possession.* For an occupancy or possession to exist, must have a definite period at which it commenced; and when should this be? As soon as the author conceived the ideas, or not till he had written them down, or not till he had published them? In the first two cases, it was absurd to assert that he could thus have a right to prevent others, to whom they might equally occur, from publishing them; and in the last, it seemed strange to date the *private* property from the time of making them *public.* Besides, many might never see the book; and surely the ideas were as free to them to publish, as to the original parties. It had no *distinguishable proprietary marks:* for what stamp or token of property could a man affix to intellectual ideas: how signify to the world that he had appropriated them to himself; since mere mental ideas admit not of any actual or visible possession? And it could not be the subject of *sole and exclusive enjoyment.* For an author to have this, although he need not have total actual possession in himself, must have the *potential* power, that is, the power of confining it to himself and excluding others. Now an author could not be said to exercise this power over his ideas after publication. And it was no sign, as it was contended, that an author had a property in his works, because he had the 'jus fruendi, ac disponendi;' for that definition of property merely relates to the *personal dominion* of a proprietor, and not to the *object;* and respects an *acknowledged* subject of property, not the object which is *presumed* to be so.

And, secondly, that if such a right could exist, yet there was no legal proof that it did; for the only evidences in favour of a common-law right by custom before the statute of Anne, besides some injunctions of the Court of Chancery, were two by-laws of the Stationers' Company, which applied exclusively to their own members, and some ordinances and particular privileges, made at a time when might had more sway than right. Therefore, to deduce a custom in favour of Copyright from proofs of this nature, was as absurd as if it had been contended, that there was a right to search houses, seize books, and imprison persons, because formerly such a right was sanctioned by those acts. Again, those acts, even allowing their validity, did not strictly apply, for there was no mention of the *author* in them ; all the protections, all the rights, were conferred on *printers.* In fact, the ordinances and acts were all calculated with political views, and the protection they gave was only *incidentally* to members of the Stationers' Company and patentees, and not to the rights of authors in general.

As to the injunctions of the Court of Chancery, except in three cases, one of Nelson's Fasts and Festivals, another of the Whole Duty of Man, and a third of Newton's Milton's Paradise Lost, they were not granted by virtue of any supposed common-law right, but under the provisions of the 8 of Anne, c. 19: for by this act, there was certainly a sufficient property during the term thereby secured, on which to found an application for an injunction; since the statute in the first place, and before the penal provisions, affirmatively enacts, that the author or his assigns shall have the sole right of printing, for the terms therein mentioned, and then ordains penalties in case of disobedience; so that there is a distinct *right* given to the *author* and his assigns, whilst the *penalty* is given to the *informer* and the Crown in equal parts. And Lord Chief Justice Holt lays it down, "that wherever a statute gives a right, the party shall by consequence have an action at law to recover it."* The author's remedy is very different from an informer's prosecuting for

* Ewer *v.* Jones, 2 Salk. 415 and 6 Mod. 26.

the penalty. The latter must pursue all the remedies the statute requires; for in such a prosecution, the charge is for an *offence*, and therefore the offence must be ***strictly brought within*** all the provisions of the act. But if the plaintiff only seeks satisfaction to himself as the *party aggrieved*, without prosecuting for any penalty, there is not in such case any limitation by the statute.* And as to the three excepted cases of injunctions, had they even been perpetual, instead of being only temporary as they were, they could have no effect in a court of common law, in a common-law case; and although it was urged that they were acquiesced under, yet the acquiescence of parties could not alter the law, and these injunctions were but temporary suspensions, 'till the rights should be determined;' and none of them contain any express *decision* whatever. For the Court of Chancery evidently considered this matter as unsettled, since in the case of Millar against Donaldson, Lord Northington would not determine the point, but left it to be considered in a court of common law. And with regard to the case of Milton's Paradise Lost, there is a note of Lord Hardwick's, by which it seems that the injunction in that case was founded on Dr. Newton's notes only; for his Lordship said, "that at first he was inclined to send the cause to the Judges to settle the point of law; but as Dr. Newton's notes were *manifestly within* 8 Anne, he would grant an injunction to them, without deciding the *general* question of property at *common* law."

And, thirdly, that if there was proof that such a property did once exist, yet the statute 8 of Anne, c. 19, had taken it away, and on principles of public policy it ought not to be again revived. The act is entitled, "An Act for the Encouragement of Learning:" and how?—"By vesting the copies of printed books in the authors or purchasers of such copies, during the times therein mentioned." But had they had a right

* See the case of Beckford *v.* Hood, post. p. 56.

at common law before; it would have been a strange *encouragement* 'to *abridge* an actual right before subsisting in them; to *deprive* them (as was done by the 4th section, which regulated the price of books) of the natural right (which every other person has) of fixing the price of the goods he sells, and to subject the value of their *property* to the regulation of *others.*' Besides, 'the penalty does not seem much calculated for "the encouragement" of the author; for the books are to be forthwith damasked, and made waste paper of, and the forfeiture is to go, one half to the king, the other to the informer, but no part of it to the author.' It was clear, then, by the change made in the bill, from "securing the property," to "vesting the copies," that it appeared 'to the legislature that abstractedly from this statute, authors had no *exclusive right* whatever; and consequently, must be very far from having any pretensions to an *eternal monopoly:* but that, as the act gave them a temporary monopoly for a limited time, it might be reasonable to make the provisions and restrictions contained in it; and they would then have a proper operation.' And that as to the provision in the 9th section, "That nothing in this act should extend to any right that the Universities or any persons have in any book already printed, or after to be printed," which, it was contended, excepted the common-law right of the author; it was plain to see, that it had no view to any general question of law or general claim; but was only pointed at the printing and reprinting of particular books. For if the design of the statute clearly was to vest a temporary copyright in the author, what a laborious nullity it would have been, after all, to say, that the foregoing enactments were not to have any effect on the possessions of authors.

And on principles of public policy, such a claim should not be allowed, when the inconveniences were seen, which might ensue from it. For it would be in the power of booksellers or others, who had purchased the works of our best authors, to wholly suppress them: and although it was said, that if they did not keep a sufficient number of copies in hand, it would amount to an abandonment of their right, and any might print them; yet who was to say, what was an abandonment, and what endless litigation it might lead to? And as to prices, a bookseller might ask what prices he pleased for useful works, and so the generality of mankind be debarred of their use, which was the purpose of their publication.

And, in truth, the only claim 'an author can *really* make, is to the *public benevolence*, by way of encouragement. For his case is exactly similar to that of an inventor of a new machine. Both original inventions stand upon the same footing in point of property; whether the case be *mechanical* or *literary*, whether it be an *Epic Poem* or an *Orrery*. Mr. Harrison, the inventor of the Time-piece, employed at least as much time and labour and study upon his time-keeper, as Mr. Thomson could do in writing his Seasons: for in planning that machine, all the faculties of the mind must have been fully exerted. And as far as value is a mark of property, Mr. Harrison's time-piece was, surely, as valuable in itself, as Mr. Thomson's Seasons. And yet it is on all sides acknowledged, whenever a machine is published, (be it ever so useful and ingenious) the inventor has no right to it, but only by patent; which can only give him a temporary privilege. And although the inventor of the air-pump had certainly a property in the *machine* which he formed, he did not thereby gain the sole property in the *abstract principles* upon which he constructed his machine: and yet these might well be called the inventor's ideas, and as much his sole property as the ideas of an author.'

Therefore, on the whole, inasmuch 'as the monopoly now claimed was contrary to the great laws of property, and totally unknown to the ancient and common-law of England: as the establishing of this claim would directly contradict the legislative authority, and introduce a species of property contrary to the end for which the whole system of property was established: as it would tend to embroil the peace of society, with frequent contentions—(contentions most highly disfiguring the face of literature, and highly disgusting to a liberal mind): as it would hinder and suppress the advancement of learning and knowledge; and as it would strip the subject of his natural rights;' it was hoped that the Court would at once disallow so extravagant a claim.

In answer to these arguments, the supporters of the claim of literary property replied, first, that the metaphysical reasonings concerning the notions of property, indulged in by their opponents, were too subtile: That their definitions of property were too narrow and too confined; for the rules attending property must keep pace with its increase and improvement, and must be adapted to every case: That a distinguishable existence in the thing claimed as property, an actual value in that thing to the true owner, are its essentials: That the best rule of reason and justice seemed to be, 'to assign to everything capable of ownership, a legal and determinate owner:' That it was not necessary that the subject should be of utility to man, or have any capacity to be fastened on, as was insisted: That a capacity to be distinguished answered every end of reason and certainty, which is the great favorite of the law: That "the present claim was founded upon the original right to the work, as being the mental labour of the author; and that the effect and produce of the labour was his: That it was a personal incorporeal property, saleable and profitable, having 'indicia certa;' for though the sentiments and doctrines might be called ideal, yet when the same were communicated to the sight and understanding of every man by the medium of printing, the work became a distinguishable subject of property, and not totally destitute of corporeal qualities:" That indeed to contend otherwise was futile, since it was settled and admitted that literary compositions in their original state, and incorporeal right of the publication of them were the private and exclusive property of the author, and that they might be ever retained so; and that if they were ravished from him before publication, trover or trespass lay.* Now how should the jury estimate the damages in such a case? By the value of the ink and paper? 'Certainly not. It would be most reasonable to consider the known character and ability of the author, and the value which his work (so taken from him), would produce by the publication and sale. But without publication, the work would be useless to the author, because without profit, and property without the power of use and disposal, is an empty sound. Publication, therefore, is the necessary act, and only means, to render this confessed property useful to mankind, and profitable to the owner; in this they are jointly concerned.' It would be therefore harsh and unreasonable to construe this only and necessary act to make the work useful and profitable, to be destructive at once of the author's confessed original property, against his expressed will. That to contend 'that by the law of nature, property ends when corporeal possession ceases,' was clearly false, since Barbeyrac shows, that such perpetual possession is impossible, and that however 'we may presume this in respect to those things which remain such as nature has produced them; yet, as for other things which are the fruits of human industry, and which are done with great labour and contrivance usually, it cannot be doubted but every one would preserve his right to them till he makes an open renunciation.'† Now there was no open renunciation in the present case, for was there not a difference betwixt selling the property in the work, and only one of the copies? 'Could it be conceived, that in purchasing a literary composition at

* Pope *v.* Curl. Webb *v.* Rose. Lord Clarendon's Works. Forrester *v.* Walker. Duke of Queensbury *v.* Shebbeare.

† Ed. of *Puffendorf.* Lib. iv c. 6. note 1.

a shop, the purchaser ever thought he bought the right to be the printer and seller of that specific work? The improvement, knowledge, or amusement which he could derive from the performance was all his own, but the right to the work, the Copyright, remained to him whose industry composed it.'

With regard to the second head or division of the defendant's argument, namely, that there was no legal proof of the existence of Copyright before the 8th of Anne, c. 19, it was answered that the exclusive privileges, the decrees of Star-chamber, and the ordinances of Parliament, were legal proofs to the extent to which they were cited, for they were not adduced as acts *establishing* a right, but merely as *recognitions* of one previously existing; that further confirmations of this right were to be found in the customs of the Stationers' Company. And although it was said that these customs and by-laws were inconclusive in proof of a general usage, inasmuch as they were only binding on their own members, yet, in thus arguing, it seemed to be totally forgotten that *all printers* were obliged to belong to the Stationers' Company; and although perhaps there might be always some unallowed printing going on secretly, yet such was an exception to the general rule, and could in no way impugn a general usage. That as to no mention of the author ever being made, but only the printer, it was quite clear that this arose from the printer generally standing 'in loco auctoris,' being the 'owner' of the copy; whilst the author from various circumstances, either from inability of means, or want of confidence of success, seldom took upon himself the risk of publishing on his own account; but that when he did so, he came under the words 'owner of a copy,' and so was protected.

As to the injunctions of the Court of Chancery, all the cases went to prove, that that Court had treated the 8th of Anne, c. 19, as merely confirming and securing antecedent property for a limited term, without prejudice to the common-law right; for if that Court had founded their injunctions, as it was contended, on the statute right, it would have been necessary, under the section which provides, 'That all actions, suits, bills, &c., for any offence that shall be committed against this act, shall be brought, sued, and commenced *within three months* after the offence committed;' that the bill should be brought within three months, which was not however the case. But there were some cases of injunctions, which could not by any stretch of argument be supposed to have been granted under the authority of the 8th of Anne. There was the case of 'Nelson's Fasts and Festivals,' where an injunction was acquiesced under in 1736, for a work published in 1703, the author having died in 1714; and that of 'The Whole Duty of Man,' where the injunction was acquiesced under in 1735, and the original assignment had been made in 1657. There was also the case of Motte *v.* Falkner, for printing Pope and Swift's Miscellanies, where the injunction was granted in 1735, and some of the pieces were printed in 1701 and 1702; and yet the Court granted the injunction to the whole, although the counsel for the defendant strongly pressed the objection as to those pieces; and Falkner was a man of substance, and the general point was of consequence to him, yet he was advised to acquiesce under the injunction. As to the case of the "Paradise Lost," it must be observed that Lord Hardwick, although indeed he guarded himself from giving an opinion on the general question, would hardly have granted the injunction, and penned it himself to the whole and in the disjunctive, so that printing the poem, or the life, or Bentley's notes, without one word of Dr. Newton's, would have been a breach, if he had not had a strong leaning in favour of the plaintiff's case. That although it was true, that these decisions in Chancery were not authorities in a common-law Court; yet they were competent as proofs of the opinion of the Court of Chancery in favour of an acknowledged copyright, pre-existing and independent of the statute of Anne. With respect to the case of Millar *v.* Donaldson, which was cited as proof of a doubt arising in the Chancery Court as to this common-law right, Lord Northington, on that occasion, refused an injunction, because the precise question of law was at that moment pending in the Exchequer, in the case of Tonson against Collins, and as his Lordship very properly observed, it would have been presumption in him to have given an opinion, when the question of law was then in course of trial before the proper tribunal.

And a still more convincing proof of a previously existing common-law right, was afforded by the statute itself; for it was applied for, on the ground that an action on the case not being a sufficient protection for copyrights, the legislature would therefore be pleased to enact penalties and forfeiture of pirated books, which shows clearly that at the time of passing the statute, an action on the case was held to be the acknowledged remedy for infringement of a right that must before then have existed. And that such was the case, and such the light in which it was viewed by the legislature, is apparent from the wording of the act. For would the act, if it had been establishing a new and unheard of right till that time, have recited, "Whereas printers, &c., *have of late frequently taken the liberty of printing*, &c., without the consent of the authors or proprietors, &c., *to their very great detriment, and too often to the ruin of their families.*" Is not this a description of some infringement of a previously existing right, which had *of late* grown to that excess as to require by its ruinous consequences the interference of the legislature? The Act continues, "For preventing therefore the like *practices* for the future :" would the word "*practices*" have been used to describe a legal right (which the reprinting of books would have been, when there was no copyright,) or is it not rather fitted to express acts committed in fraud and violation of private rights, which this act was made to prevent?

And with regard to the third and last division of the

defendant's argument; it was denied that the statute 8th of Anne, did abrogate any common-law right, that might before have existed. Looking at the statute itself, and the circumstances under which it was passed, it was clear that it was only intended to give *a further remedy* in the shape of penalties and forfeitures, which were to be in force for a limited period, and to recover which, it was necessary so far to publish the ownership of the work, by entry in the Stationers' books, that no one might offend through ignorance. The proviso at the end was meant to prevent any misconception of the effect of the statute on the author's common-law right; for the words "any right," manifestly mean any other right than the term secured by the act, and the act speaks of no right whatsoever but that of authors, or derived from them; therefore, no other right could possibly be prejudiced or confirmed by any expression in the act, such as prerogative copies or patents, to which, as it was objected, these words referred. As to the clause respecting the price of books, although the inference drawn from it, as to the intention of the framers of the bill, was ingenious, it could not hold good; as the clause referred to *all* books, was perpetual, and was indeed only a revival of the 25 Hen. VIII. c. XV. sec. 4, which was never repealed till the 12 Geo. II.

As to the comparison between a literary and a mechanical work, it was thus answered: that they were of very different natures, for "the property of the maker of a mechanical engine is confined to that individual thing which he has made; and the machine made in imitation or resemblance of it is a different work in substance, materials, labour, and expense in which the maker of the original machine cannot claim any property; for it is not his, but only a resemblance of his; whereas the reprinted book is the very same substance, because its doctrine and sentiments are its essential and substantial part, and the printing of it is a mere mechanical act, and the method only of publishing and promulging the contents of the book."

And in answer to those arguments, which went to prove that such a claim ought not to be encouraged, it was contended, that it was not agreeable to natural justice that a stranger should reap the beneficial pecuniary produce of another man's work; "Jure naturæ æquum est, neminem cum alterius detrimento et injuriâ fieri locupletiorem:" That it was wise for every State to encourage letters, and the painful researches of learned men: That the easiest and most equal way of doing it, was by securing to them the property of their own works: That no one contributes who is not willing; and though a good work may be run down, and a bad one cried up for a time, yet sooner or later the reward will be in proportion to the merit of the work: That a writer's fame would not be the less that he has bread, without being under the necessity of prostituting his pen to flattery or party to get it: That he who engages in a laborious work, (such, for instance, as Johnson's Dictionary,) which may employ his whole life, will do it with more spirit, if, besides his own glory, he thinks it may be a provision for his family: That the fear of books being suppressed was chimerical; and as to their price being enhanced, it was equally so; for whilst an author might make additions and corrections to his work, highly valuable, he would always find it his interest to prevent the charge from becoming unreasonable; since a small profit in a speedy and numerous sale, is much larger gain than a great profit upon each book in a slow sale of less number.

Therefore, it was contended, that "on every principle of reason, natural justice, morality, and common law; on the evidence of the long received opinion of this property, appearing in ancient proceedings, and in law cases; on the clear sense of the legislature, and the opinions of the greatest lawyers of their time in the Court of Chancery, since that statute; the right of an author to the copy of his works was well-founded;" and it was hoped, "that the learned and industrious would be permitted from thenceforth, not only to reap the fame, but the profits of their ingenious labours without interruption, to the honour and advantage of themselves and their families, and the increase and promotion of the interests of literature."

These last reasons appeared so convincing to three out of the four Judges who heard the cause, one of whom was Lord Mansfield, that judgment was pronounced in favour of the plaintiff; and although a writ of error was afterwards brought, the plaintiff in error suffered himself to be non-prossed; and the Lords Commissioners, after Trinity Term, 1770, granted an injunction.

CHAPTER IX.

FROM THE DECISION IN THE CASE OF MILLAR AGAINST TAYLOR IN 1769, TO THAT OF BECKFORD AGAINST HOOD, 1798.

THE security and protection given by the foregoing decision to Copyright property, did not, however, long continue; for in a case that arose soon afterwards, where judgment was given on the authority of the foregoing decision, the defendant was advised to try an appeal to the House of Lords,* on which occasion the following questions were propounded to the Judges:—

"1. Whether at common law, an author of any book or literary composition, had the sole right of first printing and publishing the same for sale, and might bring an action against any person who printed, published, and sold the same without his consent?

"2. If the author had such right originally, did the law take it away upon his printing and publishing such book or literary composition; and might any person afterwards reprint and sell, for his own benefit, such book or literary composition, against the will of the author?

"3. If such action would have lain at common law, is it taken away by the statute of 8 Anne? And is an author by the said statute precluded from every remedy, except on the

* Donaldson *v.* Becket and others, in 1774, 2 Bro. P. C. 129, 4 Burr. Rep. p. 2408.

foundation of the said statute, and on the terms and conditions prescribed thereby?"

And after time being given to consider, they delivered their opinions seriatim; and there were of the eleven Judges, eight to three for the affirmative on the first question; four to seven on the second; and six to five on the third; so that it was concluded, that although an author by common law had an exclusive right to print his works, and did not lose it by the mere act of publication, yet the statute of 8 Anne, c. 19, had completely deprived him of that right. Lord Mansfield did not, out of delicacy, (as it is unusual for a Peer to support his own judgment) deliver any opinion; but it is well known that he concurred with the eight upon the first question, with the seven on the second, and with the five upon the third. Justice Blackstone was one of the majority on the two first questions, and of the minority on the third.

So that this opinion of the Judges, as to the 8 of Anne taking away the right at common law, was only carried by a majority of one out of the eleven; and had delicacy permitted Lord Mansfield to support his own decision, the Judges would have been equally divided. Besides, of the six Judges who decided that the 8 of Anne had taken away the common law right of the author, there was one who was of opinion, that the author had not the sole right of first printing and publishing his work, and could not maintain an action against those who did so without his consent; two who held, that although the author had this right, he could not maintain any action, unless it were taken from him by fraud or violence; and a fourth, who considered, that although an author had the sole right of first printing and publishing, and could maintain an action for its infringement; yet the moment he elected to publish, he abandoned this right, and any one might reprint the same: so that there were *only two* out of the six, that actually considered the point of the 8 of Anne taking away a previously existing right, the other four not agreeing that there was any such previous right.

But, doubtful therefore as this opinion may well be considered, it was a judgment on an appeal to the highest tribunal the law recognizes, and as such was esteemed practically decisive of the point—that any common-law right the author might before have had, was taken away by the 8 of Anne.

The result of this trial, when known, so alarmed the trade, by the serious consequences of it on their property, that they immediately presented a petition to the House of Commons,* setting forth 'that they had constantly apprehended that the 8 of Anne, c. 19, did not interfere with any Copyright that might be invested in the petitioners by common law; and that they had therefore, for many years past, continued to purchase and sell such Copyrights, in the same manner as if such act had never been made: That the petitioners were confirmed in such their apprehensions, in regard that no determination was had during the period limited by the said act, in prejudice of such common-law right; and the same was recognised by a judgment in the Court of King's Bench, in Easter, 1769; that in consequence thereof many thousand pounds had been at different times invested in the purchase of ancient Copyrights, not protected by the statute 8 of Anne, so that the support of many families in a great measure depended upon the same; that, by a late decision of the House of Peers, such common-law right of authors and their assigns had been declared to have no existence, whereby the petitioners would be very great sufferers through their former voluntary misapprehension of the law; and therefore praying the House to take their singularly hard case into consideration, and to grant them such relief in the premises as to the House should seem meet.'

* On the 28th of February, 1774.

A committee was accordingly appointed, and on the 24th of March, 1774, they gave in their report, in which they referred to evidence laid before them of the practice and belief of the trade as to a common-law right, till the recent decision in the House of Peers; and of the immediate depreciation in the value of Copyrights which had ensued from that decision. Leave was accordingly given to bring in "a Bill for relief of booksellers and others, by vesting the copies of printed books in the purchasers of such copies from authors or their assigns, for a time therein to be limited."

It was taken up to the House of Lords on the 31st of May, but on the 2nd of June, on its being read a first time, it was moved that it be read a second time that day two months. A debate thereupon ensued.

'Lord Lyttleton was for its being read a second time, and said that he had letters from Dr. Robertson, Mr. Hume, &c., in favour of the Bill, and that the price the booksellers gave for Hawkesworth's voyage, was proof that they did believe they had a common-law right. That this Bill was not to repeal that decision which the house had come to, but to relieve men who had laid out about £60,000 in Copyright since the year 1769.' He also said in the course of his speech: 'Authors are not to be denied a free participation of the common rights of mankind, and their property is surely as sacred and deserving protection as that of any other subject.'

Lord Camden, however, urged, 'that they never could suppose they had a common-law right, for that it was first supported by Star Chamber decrees; that when they obtained the Act of the 8th of Anne, they could not suppose it, for the advantage and security of that Act were far short of what the common-law afforded them, had their claims been defensible on that ground; that on the expiration of the monopoly, in 1731, they could not fall into such a mistake, for they applied to Parliament for an extension of the monopoly in the years 1735, 6, and 7;* and that he could not but think this attempt an affront on the house, viewed with regard to their recent decision.'

Lord Denbigh and Lord Apsley (the Lord Chancellor) also spoke against it. Lord Mansfield was not present during the debate. The house then divided, and the motion was carried by a majority of 21 to 11; so the bill was never further proceeded with. The account of the debate is very meagre, and we cannot learn what were the precise provisions of the bill; but it would appear that it was not founded on any general principles, but had only a limited application to Copyrights then in being.

Alarmed by the recent decision, the Universities applied to Parliament for protection of their Copyrights; and these powerful bodies, allied as they were to both houses by ties and associations, perhaps the strongest and most lasting of the kind that occur in a man's life, had no difficulty in obtaining that justice for themselves which was sternly denied to the owners of Copyright at large.

The 15 of Geo. III, c. 53, was passed, which enables the Universities and the Colleges of Eton, Westminster, and Winchester, to hold in perpetuity the Copyright in all works already given, or which might hereafter be given them under similar penalties, as in the 8 of Anne.

It appeared that it had been for some time the practice with booksellers, in order to evade what they considered the oppressive tax of giving in nine copies for the public libraries, to enter only the title of the first volume of their works in the register book; and then the public libraries could only claim a single volume, which of course was useless, and seldom demanded. To remedy this, a clause was inserted in the above act, that no penalties under the 8th of Anne should

* Lord Camden seems to have mistaken the object of those applications to Parliament. See ante p. 37, 8.

accrue, unless the title to the whole copy of a work, and every volume thereof, should be entered in the register book of the Stationers' Company; and unless nine copies of it were actually delivered to the warehouse-keeper of the Company for the use of the libraries in that act mentioned.*

By this we may clearly see the high favor in which the Universities stood, when they not only procured a statute conferring especial protection on their Copyrights, but also procured a confirmation of their claim to a gratuitous copy of each work that was published by others who enjoyed no such privilege. But the effect of this latter concession did not answer its expectation; for several booksellers preferred losing the protection afforded by the 8th of Anne altogether, by not entering their works in the register book, to delivering nine copies gratuitously of expensive and costly works: and of this more hereafter.

In 1798, a point, which was incidentally touched on in the foregoing case of Millar against Taylor, namely, whether the author had any right conferred by the 8th of Anne, beyond the remedies specifically pointed out by that act, came before the Court of King's Bench, in the case of Beckford against Hood, † which was an action on the case for damages brought by the author of a book for pirating it, during the 28 years given by the Statute. And three points were made; 1st. That no action for damages would lie since the 8th of Anne; 2ndly. That if it would lie, the provision in the statute which requires the entry at Stationers' Hall, must be duly complied with; And 3rdly, That the plaintiff had abandoned his property in it, by publishing it anonymously. But it was decided, on the principle laid down by Mr. Justice Yates, in the case of Millar against Taylor,‡ that, by the first section of the 8th of Anne, the author had an absolute right for a term of years, sufficient to support an action on the

* Sec. vi.

† 7 Term. Rep. 620.

‡ 4 Burr. Rep. pp. 2380, 1; and see Ante, pp. 44, 5.

case: * that by the interpretation given to the clause requiring the entry, by the 6th section of the 15th Geo. III. c. 53, it was clear that the entry was only requisite to entitle a party to the penalties; and with regard to the not affixing a name to the publication, that such an omission could not be looked on but by the utmost casuistry, as a purposed abandonment of a preceding right.

The Court, in this case, felt the difficulty in which they were placed by the decision in the House of Lords, on the appeal of Donaldson against Beckett and others, for they were bound to construe the statute 8 of Anne, c. 19, as taking away a previously existing common-law right of the author; and yet they could not conceal from themselves, the injustice of such a construction, or reconcile it to the express language of the act. 'They could not find in this act,' they said, 'the encouragement which the statement in the recital held out to authors. The supposed remedy was wholly inadequate to the purpose: it only gave penalties and forfeiture; and even those not to the author, but to any who might preoccupy his place by first suing.' They were therefore obliged to put what may almost be termed a forced construction on the first section, to supply the remedy they felt to be necessary, and which they in vain sought for in the express provisions of the act. †

* This decision seemed contrary to that in Donaldson *v.* Beckett and others, where five out of the six Judges, (all that considered this point) held that an author "was precluded from every remedy, except on the foundation of the statute, and *on the terms and conditions prescribed thereby*." But Mr. Justice Grose in this case said, with reference to that decision, that "the amount of their opinions only went to establish that the common-law right of action could not be exercised *beyond the time limited* by that statute."

† This fact alone seems to me a stronga rgument that the 8th of Anne, c. 19, did not take away the author's pre-existing common-law right.

thors for that purpose, which the public at large did not bear. There were many works which cost 50 guineas a copy, and was it not monstrous that the authors and publishers should be taxed to the amount of 550 guineas, by being obliged to give away 11 copies? The fact was, that such works, from the expense attending them, were in no danger of being pirated; no person being able to enter into competition with them, or to deprive them of the benefit of Copyright therein. There were other books, however, of great sale and merit, though cheap, to which the contribution of eleven copies would be easy; but he should certainly propose that expensive works, when the publishers were not anxious about their Copyright, should be exempted from this contribution.'

It was contended, however, that it was only a confirmation of the Act of Queen Anne, which had not been acted on of late years, in consequence of a doubt being suggested in point of law, as to the efficacy of the Act itself. Mr. Abercromby proposed that the period of Copyright should be limited to 20 years, instead of 28. Mr. Morris insisted, 'that the term of 28 years was not too much for a just Copyright; he cited the cases of Dr. Adam Smith's works, and Dr. Johnson's Dictionary, to prove that most valuable works were not properly estimated till they had gone through many editions, and had been long before the public.' Some further conversation having taken place, the house was resumed, and the further consideration of the report ordered for the 24th instant.

However, it appeared to be a general feeling that it was too late in the Session to proceed further with this Bill, for we hear nothing more of it between this time and the prorogation of Parliament, which took place on the 4th of July. And when Parliament met again, Mr. Villiers, in the meantime, having been sent as Ambassador to Portugal, the subject was not resumed.

Thus matters remained in the same state, until in 1811 Professor Christian, who had given the point a great deal of time and attention, persuaded the University of Cambridge that the true construction of the 8th of Anne required a delivery of the eleven copies, whether the entry was made or not; and that they had a clear right at law which they might enforce. Pursuant to his advice, therefore, they brought an action against a bookseller of the name of Bryer, for not delivering a copy of a work he had printed, although he had not entered the title; and the Court of King's Bench decided in favour of Professor Christian's construction. *

Soon after this decision a motion was made for an amendment of the law on this subject; and as the former motion by Mr. Villiers was to procure for the Universities a recognition of a privilege which they did not enjoy, so the present one, by Mr. Giddy, was to procure for authors and booksellers an enactment destructive of that privilege, which the recent decision in the King's Bench had now enabled the Universities to enforce. And as on Mr. Villiers' motion the House was advised not to meddle with the matter, since they had no petitions from parties interested in it; so on the present occasion the motion was prefaced by the introduction of a petition by Mr. Giddy, † from the booksellers and publishers of London and Westminster, complaining of the clause, and showing the hardship in the case of expensive works, of which only a limited number of copies were printed. They also complained of the further term of 14 years, being dependant on the author's being alive at the end of the first, 'which,' say they, 'is a distinction in many cases productive of great hardships to the families of authors, and is not founded on just principles.'

On the 11th of March, 1813, another petition to the same

* Univ. of Cambr. *v.* Bryer. 16 East. p. 317.

† On the 16th of Dec. 1812.

effect was produced from several printers of London and Westminster, and Mr. Giddy thereupon moved "that a committee be appointed to examine the Acts relating to Copyright, and to report, whether any and what alterations were requisite to be made therein." A short discussion ensued, in the course of which Sir Samuel Romilly, in answer to some observations, said: "There is another mistake under which the honourable gentleman" (referring to a member who had previously spoken) "labours, in supposing that the act of Queen Anne conferred a benefit on authors; no such thing. Before the passing of that act, authors had the exclusive property in their works; and the act in question went to limit that right to 14 years in the first instance, and to another period of 14 years, if the author should be alive at the expiration of the first period. The only privilege conferred by this act, which authors did not before enjoy, went to some penalties which were immaterial. It operated in a way most injurious to the best interests of literature, for as young authors were more likely to reach the second term than old, it gave the immature and jejune compositions of the former, double the reward reserved for the productions of ripened genius."

A committee was accordingly appointed, and on the 17th of June, they gave in their report, by which they recommended some changes and alterations in the law respecting the delivery of copies to the public libraries, and concluded thus: "Lastly, your committee have taken into their consideration the subject of Copyright, which extends at present to 14 years certain, and then to a second period of equal duration, provided the author happens to survive the first. They are inclined to think that no adequate reason can be given for this contingent reversion, and that a fixed term should be assigned beyond the existing period of 14 years."

Nothing more was done this session; but in the ensuing one, on the 10th of May, 1814, Mr. Giddy moved for and obtained leave to bring in, pursuant to the report of that committee, "A Bill to amend the several acts for the encouragement of learning, by securing the copies and Copyright of printed books to the authors of such books and their assigns."

On the 18th May, on the house resolving pro formâ into a committee, Mr. Giddy stated shortly the heads of his Bill as follows: "1. That it should not be necessary that the copies of books presented to the public libraries, should be on fine paper. 2. That no books need be presented to these libraries, unless such as were required from the booksellers. 3. That all Copyrights should be entered at Stationers' Hall; and that if the author, by a special entry, waived his Copyright, he should then only be required to present one copy to the British Museum. 4. That the term of Copyright be extended from 14 years certain, and another 14 years if the author was living at the end of the first term, to 28 years certain." And another clause to prevent the copies presented to the libraries from being afterwards sold, which, it was alleged, was often done.

This bill was very near being again postponed to another session; but on the 18th of July several amendments having been discussed and carried,* the bill was ordered to be read a third time the next day, which was done, some further amendments made, and the bill passed and sent up to the Lords.

The Lords passed the bill with two amendments, which

* In the course of the discussion, Sir Egerton Brydges gave notice that he would next day "move for an amendment in the bill to extend further the period of copyright." Whether he did so or not, does not appear; as there is no account of the debate that took place on the 19th. The discussion on the 18th was principally as to the hardship or expediency of the clause, providing certain copies to be given to public libraries; and Mr. Marsh presented a petition to the House from a gentleman of the name of Fisher, "who, it appeared, had travelled all over Great Britain for the purpose of collecting specimens of painting, architecture, and the arts, for the purpose of

were sections 8 and 9, by which a partially retrospective effect was given to the further term of copyright created by the Act; and the Commons, on the 27th of July, agreeing to those amendments, the bill on the 29th received the royal assent.

This Act, which stands in the Statute-Book as the 54 Geo. III., c. 156, repeals so much of the 8 of Anne, and the 41 Geo. III., c. 107, as requires the absolute delivery of eleven copies of every book published, of the best paper; and instead thereof, enacts, for the future, that the copies shall only be delivered, on demand in writing being made, and with the exception of the one for the British Museum, shall be of that paper, on which the largest number of such book shall be imprinted for sale. Penalty, for not delivering copy according to demand £5, over and above the value of the copy, and full costs of suit; to be recovered in an action of debt, or other proper action, in any court of record.

And after reciting the term of copyright created by 8th of Anne, and confirmed by 41 Geo. III., and that "it would afford further encouragement to literature, if the duration of such copyright were extended in the manner thereinafter mentioned;" it enacts 'that in future the term of copyright shall be for twenty-eight years certain, and if the author be living at the expiration of that time, till his death; under pain of an action on the case for damages, with double costs of suit; copies of books to be forfeited and made waste paper of; and a penalty of 3d. per sheet, half to the Crown, and half to the informer.'

The title of all works, except Magazines, &c., (the entry of the first number of which will suffice,) to be entered in the register-book of the Stationers' Company, under penalty

afterwards publishing them with plates and illustrations; but who, having finished his work with respect to one county only, Bedford, was deterred by the great expense of the work, and the necessity of presenting the public libraries with eleven copies of it, from proceeding further."

of £5, and eleven times the value of the work; with a proviso that a want of such entry shall not forfeit copyright, but only subject to penalty.

Sections 8 and 9 give living authors of works published at the time of passing the act a further modified interest in the copyright, under certain circumstances*; and section 10 limits the time of bringing actions, &c., for offences against this act to one twelvemonth.†

In 1819 a point was made, whether by the wording of this act, the author of a piece first published in manuscript, did not lose his copyright; for that the statute made the printing a condition precedent. But Chief Justice Abbott decided, "that the above statute must be construed with reference to the 8th of Anne, c. 19, which it recites, and which, together with the 41 Geo. III., c. 107, were all made, 'in pari materiâ,' for the purpose of enlarging the rights of authors; that the 8th of Anne, c. 19, gave to authors a copyright in works not only composed and printed, but composed and not printed; and that he thought it was not the intention of the legislature either to abridge authors of any of their

* In 1818, a question arose as to the construction of these clauses; and it was decided by the Court of King's Bench, (Brooke *v.* Clarke, 1 B & A. 396) that these clauses gave authors who had published their works less than fourteen years before the passing of that act, an absolute term of fourteen years, after the expiration of the first fourteen years; and to authors who had published their works less than twenty-eight years before that act, the copyright for their life. But where the interest was not in the author, or his assigns, by the existing law, at the passing of the act, then it did not re-create a term, for the whole intention of the act was merely to extend it. And this decision was agreeable to common justice; for where the author's right had expired before the passing of the act, some third parties might have undertaken to print it, and it would have been hard upon them to revive the copyright, which they had concluded as ended.

† This act is the one now in force, regulating copyright property. The only subsequent alteration is respecting the gratuitous delivery of copies to the public libraries, which by the 6th and 7th William IV., c. 110, is now limited to five copies instead of eleven.

former rights, or to impose upon them as a condition precedent, that they should not sell their compositions in manuscript before they were printed."*

* White *v.* Geroch, 2 B. & A. 298. This case is not so reported as to enable one to ascertain on what precise grounds it was contended that a '*sale* in MS.' took away the author's right by the 54 Geo. III. The word, it is conceived, ought to be a '*publication* in MS.' Even the particular words relied on in the Statute, do not seem to be given; for those that are given, do not appear to justify the conclusions sought to be drawn from them.

CHAPTER XI.

FROM THE PASSING THE 54 GEO. 3, C. 156, IN 1814, TO THE END OF THE YEAR, 1836.

In the meantime, on the 19th of June, 1817, Sir Egerton Brydges moved for leave to bring in a bill to amend the foregoing act, "so far as regards books published before the act of Queen Anne, respecting the claims to eleven copies of the said books, and also to very limited editions of books;" which, after debate, was negatived by a majority of one only: the numbers being, Ayes 57, Noes 58. * In the course of the debate, Mr. Brougham said: 'certainly the provisions of the last bill rendered it necessary to be amended, as it imposed a greater burthen on authors than they ought to bear. It certainly was not any encouragement to learning to impose on poor men the task of supplying the University with books, and thereby unnecessarily sparing the funds of those rich and well-endowed bodies.'

On the 3rd of March, in the following year, Sir E. Brydges again brought forward his motion, and the bill was allowed to be brought in, it being agreed that the opposition should be reserved for the second reading.

Numerous petitions in favour and against the bill were at various times presented. Among the rest, 'from certain au-

* Sir Egerton personally felt the hardship of this tax, in the various scarce and curious works he published at his private press at Lee Priory, Kent.

thors and composers of books,' in which the following sound and forcible remarks occur.* "The petitioners humbly submit, that in this great commercial and wealthy country, reputation alone cannot be a sufficient stimulus to authors to compose or publish valuable works, and more especially those which involve much expense; the affluence of the country operates not only to make the annual expenditure for subsistence considerable, but also to enhance the charges of every publication; the same prosperity of the country leading to costly habits of living, prevents men of literary reputation from holding the same rank in this country that it obtains in some others; justice also to the family who have to derive their nurture and respectability from the parental labours, compels the parent to devote some portion of his attention to pecuniary considerations; hence an author can rarely write for fame alone, and every subtraction from his profit, and every measure that will diminish his ardour to prepare, and the readiness of booksellers to publish his work, especially as so many require such large sums to be expended and risked upon them, is an injury, not only to authors, but to literature itself. That not only great national celebrity arises from superior excellence in works of art and literature, but it may be considered to be equally true that whatever discourages or obstructs the progress of literature in any country, will produce in time a national inferiority; and those political effects will be severely felt when they will be with much difficulty remedied."

The booksellers complained very much, and with some justice, that the libraries, with the exception of two, did not confine their demands to useful books, but exacted a copy of every work, however trifling it might be; even novels and music.†

* Presented, April 8, 1818. † Petition, 9 April, 1818.

A committee was appointedto search into the origin of this delivery of copies, and to report thereupon to the house; which they did accordingly on the 5th of June, 1818, and after tracing it from the early agreement made by Sir Thos Bodley with the Stationers' Company, through its intermediate steps, and remarking, 'that in no other country was there a demand of this nature carried to so great an extent; that in America, Prussia, Saxony, and Bavaria, one copy only was required to be deposited; in France and Austria, two; and in the Netherlands, three: but in several of these countries even this was not necessary unless Copyright was to be claimed:' They concluded by advising that this gratuitous delivery be done away with, except as regarded the British Museum; and if the Copyright be actually abandoned, then that no delivery at all should be necessary. On the report being given in, a debate arose, and it was then urged against the adoption of it, that the resolutions the committee had come to, were carried by a very slight majority; a majority of only one in one case, and of the casting vote of the Chairman in another. The Report however was ordered to be printed.

But the Parliament shortly after breaking up, nothing more was done with this bill; and when the new Parliament met on the 14th of January 1819, the subject was not again resumed, although, on the 22d of March, a petition for alteration of the existing law was presented from the booksellers, in which it was stated, "That the delivery of eleven copies of only five works, namely, 'Dugdale's Monasticon Anglicanum,' his 'History of St. Pauls,' 'Portraits of Illustrious Personages,' 'Ormerode's History of Cheshire,' and 'Wood's Athenæ Oxonienses,' would amount to £2198, 14s., and that the delivery of only one work, 'Dodwell's Scenes and Monuments of Greece,' would, at the trade price, be about £275.' The chief reason, perhaps, that the subject was not resumed, was, that its principal supporter, Sir E. Brydges, did not sit in the succeeding Parliament.

We do not find the subject again mentioned, till after a lapse of twelve years, when, on the 28th of July, 1832, Mr. Spring Rice brought forward a motion to buy up the right of the Marischal College of Aberdeen to a copy of every new work published, which they were willing to dispose of for £460 a-year; and the copies thus acquired were to be devoted to a project then afoot, of exchanging literary works with France, to which the French Government, on their part, were willing to agree. The hardship on the proprietors of Copyright, in having to furnish these eleven copies, was again referred to in the course of the debate, and a wish expressed, that some measure might be taken to do away with so oppressive and injurious a tax.

Accordingly, although this right of the Marischal College to a copy of every work was purchased, it was thought better not to execute the latter part of the project, but to give the benefit of the purchase to the booksellers, by not exacting the copy thus acquired.

In this state, matters remained till the 28th of April, 1836, when Mr. Buckingham moved for leave to bring in a bill to do away with the delivery of the eleven copies, in a speech which merely recapitulated the arguments already noticed. The bill, when brought in, remained some time in the Commons' House, but passed more quickly through the Lords, and received the Royal assent on the 20th of August, 1836.*

It enacts, that so much of the 54 of Geo. III. as relates to the delivery of a copy of every book printed to the warehouse-keepers of the Stationers' Company, for the use of the library of Zion College, the libraries of the four Universities of Scotland, and the King's Inns' Library, Dublin, should be re-

* 6 & 7 Wm. IV. c. 110.

pealed;* and it empowers the Lord Treasurer to make compensation out of the Consolidated Fund to those libraries for the loss of that privilege, which compensation is to be exclusively applied to the purchase of books.

* So that only five copies are now required to be delivered gratuitously for the use of public libraries.

CHAPTER XII.

THE MOTION OF SERGEANT TALFOURD FOR AN AMENDMENT OF THE COPYRIGHT LAWS IN 1837, AND THE PROCEEDINGS THEREON, TO THE ACCESSION OF HER PRESENT MAJESTY.

HAVING brought down this Sketch of the History of Literary Property thus far, it now remains for us to record the recent efforts which have been, and, we hope, still will continue to be made, to restore to authors and their heirs, some portion of that extended right in their works, which they possessed before the 'fatal gift' of the 8 of Anne, c. 19.

And as a question of this kind was little likely to arouse interest or awaken excitement—to confer present popularity or promise future—we must not seek for its mover amongst the leaders of party, either Ministerial or Opposition; but we must seek for one who, to great abilities should unite pure motives—who, to the voice of justice should sacrifice the cravings of ambition; one who should not only have the eloquence to persuade, but the judgment to suggest; one who, free from taint of party, might stand forth conspicuous on other grounds—on grounds of public esteem for public merit; who might advocate the claims of the great and the noble with a kindred spirit; and who, while he should have all the poet's sensibility to feel and lament the wrong, should also have all the advocate's knowledge and acuteness to propose the remedy.

Such a man was found in the author of Ion, the honourable

and learned member for Reading. In him, the rights of the greatest benefactors of mankind had an eloquent, learned, and judicious advocate.

On the 18th of May, 1837, Mr. Sergeant Talfourd moved for leave to bring in a bill to amend the law of Copyright, in a speech which was listened to by the House 'with a feeling of the most unmingled gratification.'* As the occasion is too recent to require us to enter fully into the topics of the speech, we will merely cite the following passages, giving the learned Sergeant's views on one or two points.

He thus adverts to the utter want of generous feeling they display, who seek to deprive genius of all substantial reward, because without it it will struggle for fame alone. "When the opponents of literary property speak of glory as the reward of genius, they make an ungenerous use of the very nobleness of its impulses, and show how little they have profited by its high example. When Milton, in poverty and in blindness, fed the flame of his divine enthusiasm by the assurance of a duration coequal with his language, I believe with Lord Camden that no thought crossed him of the wealth which might be amassed by the sale of his poem; but surely some shadow would have been cast upon 'the clear dream and solemn vision' of his future glories, had he foreseen that, while booksellers were striving to rival each other in the magnificence of their editions, or their adaptation to the convenience of various classes of his admirers, his only surviving descendant—a woman—should be rescued from abject want only by the charity of Garrick, who, at the solicitation of Dr. Johnson, gave her a benefit at the theatre which had appropriated to itself all that could be represented of Comus. The liberality of genius is surely ill urged for our ungrateful denial of its rights. The late Mr. Coleridge gave an example not merely of its liberality, but of its profuseness; while

* Speech of the Honourable Spring Rice.

he sought not even to appropriate to his fame the vast intellectual treasures which he had derived from boundless research, and coloured by a glorious imagination; while he scattered abroad the seeds of beauty and wisdom to take root in congenial minds, and was content to witness their fruits in the productions of those who heard him. But ought we, therefore, the less to deplore, now when the music of his divine philosophy is for ever hushed, that the earlier portion of those works on which he stamped his own impress—all which he desired of the world that it should recognize as his—are published for the gain of others than his children—that his death is illustrated by the forfeiture of their birthright? What justice is there in this? Do we reward our heroes so? Did we tell our Marlboroughs, our Nelsons, our Wellingtons, *that glory was their reward, that they fought for posterity, and that posterity would pay them?* We leave them to no such cold and uncertain requital; we do not even leave them merely to enjoy the spoils of their victories, which we deny to the author—we concentrate a nation's honest feeling of gratitude and pride into the form of an endowment, *and teach other ages what we thought, and what they ought to think* of their deeds, by the substantial memorials of our praise."

He then shows the injustice of the term of Copyright being dependent on the author's life. "There is something peculiarly unjust in bounding the term of an author's property by his natural life, if he should survive so short a period as twenty-eight years. It denies to age and experience the probable reward it permits to youth—to youth sufficiently full of hope and joy, to slight its promises. It gives a bounty to haste, and informs the laborious student who would wear away his strength to complete some work, which 'the world will not willingly let die,' that the more of his life he devotes to its perfection, the more limited shall be his interest in its fruits. It stops the progress of remuneration at the moment it is most needed, and when the benignity of nature would extract from her last calamity a means of support and comfort to survivors. At the moment when his name is invested with the solemn interest of the grave—when his eccentricities or frailties excite a smile or a shrug no longer—when the last seal is set upon his earthly course, and his works assume their place among the classics of his country—your law declares that his works shall become your property; and you requite him by seizing the patrimony of his children."—"The term allowed by the existing law is curiously adapted to encourage the lightest works, and to leave the noblest unprotected. Its little span is ample for authors who seek only to amuse; who 'to beguile the time, look like the time;' who lend to frivolity or corruption 'lighter wings to fly;' who sparkle, blaze, and expire. These may delight for a season, the fire-flies on the heaving sea of public opinion—the airy proofs of the intellectual activity of the age; yet surely it is not just to legislate for those alone, and deny all reward to that literature which aspires to endure."*

In conclusion, the learned gentleman said: "I do not in truth ask for literature favour; I do not ask for it charity; I do not even appeal to gratitude in its behalf; but I ask for it a *portion, and but a portion, of that common justice which the*

* On a subsequent occasion, on the 25th of April, 1838, he again returns to this subject, and asks—"Is there any magic in the term of twenty-eight years? Is there any conceivable principle of justice which bounds the right, if the author survives that term, by the limit of his natural life? As far as expediency shall prevail—as far as the welfare of those for whom it is the duty and the wish of the dying author to provide, may be regarded by Parliament; the period of his death is precisely that when they will most need the worldly comforts which the property in his work would confer. And as far as analogy may govern, the very attribute which induces us to regard with pride the works of intellect, is, that they survive the mortal course of those who framed them—that they are akin to what is deathless. Why should that quality render them worthless to those in whose affectionate remembrance their author still lives, while they attest a nobler immortality?"

coarsest industry obtains for its natural reward, and which nothing but the very extent of its claims, and the nobleness of the associations to which they are akin, have prevented it from receiving from our laws."

Leave was given, without one dissentient voice; and on the 6th of June accordingly, was brought in "a bill to consolidate and amend the laws relating to copyright in printed books, musical compositions, acted dramas, and engravings, to provide remedies for the violation thereof, and extend the term of its duration." As this bill has been subsequently much altered, we shall not enter into its details; but merely mention its principle, which still remains the same, and which is to extend the term of copyright, and facilitate the means afforded for its protection. The period of extension proposed is for the author's life, and the term of sixty years, to commence from the day of his death.

It was brought forward rather late in the session, and the demise of the Crown intervening, it was impossible to proceed further with it. Accordingly on the 28th of June, on the question that the bill be committed, the learned Sergeant said, that the House having recognized the principle of the bill on the second reading, it was not his intention to proceed further with it; but having received various suggestions from various quarters on the subject, he should at the next meeting of Parliament bring forward a bill, which he hoped would be still more complete in its details than the present.

CHAPTER XIII.

THE PROCEEDINGS RESPECTING THE AMENDMENT OF THE COPYRIGHT LAWS IN THE FIRST SESSION OF THE PRESENT PARLIAMENT.

Accordingly, shortly after the meeting of the new Parliament,* the learned Sergeant moved for leave to bring in a bill similar to the one of last session, for amending the law of copyright. In this bill, the clauses relating to engravings were left out, as it was intended to bring in a separate bill to amend the law respecting sculpture, and the law respecting engravings was to be included in it. So also a clause respecting international copyright was left out, as it was to be the subject of a separate bill.†

Leave was again readily and unanimously given to bring

* On the 14th of December, 1837.

† The learned Sergeant thus described the state of international copyright, in his speech on the 18th May, 1837. "At present, not only is the literary intercourse of countries, who should form one great family, degraded into a low series of mutual piracies, not only are industry and talent deprived of their just reward, but our literature is debased in the eyes of the world, by the wretched medium through which they behold it. Pilfered, and disfigured in the pilfering, the noblest images are broken, wit falls pointless, and verse is only felt in fragments of broken music:—sad fate for an irritable race! The great minds of our times have now an audience to impress far vaster than it entered into the minds of their predecessors to hope for; an audience increasing as population thickens in the cities of America, and spreads itself out through its diminishing wilds, who speak our language, and who look on our old poets as their own immortal ancestry. And if this our literature shall be theirs; if its diffusion shall follow the efforts of the stout heart and sturdy arm in their triumph over the obstacles of nature; if the woods stretching beyond their confines shall be haunted with visions of beauty which our poets have created, let those who thus are softening the rugged-

in this bill; but when it came to the second reading, a serious and formidable opposition had presented itself. There was a clause in it, providing that in cases where the author had assigned away his whole interest according to the existing law, the assignee should enjoy it for the period only that he had bought it; and that the further term of sixty years from the author's death, should revert to the author or his heirs; with a proviso, however, authorising the assignee to sell all such copies as he might have on hand at the death of the author. Now it would appear that by the practice of the trade, the term of Copyright was in reality generally prolonged beyond the legal term; no respectable publisher, from motives of mutual convenience, printing upon another. But however this might answer their purpose among themselves, and be compatible with justice and equity, as far as they were concerned, it was far otherwise with regard to the author and the public, neither of whom profited by this tacit understanding. But the publishers feeling that if this Bill were passed, they would either, in the case of a valuable work, have to purchase the remainder of the term, or be prevented on the death of an author from enjoying this implied Copyright any longer, tried every means to oppose a measure which would deprive them of this source of profit. They put forth all the arguments that could be alleged against any further prolongation; but unfortunately almost all their arguments applied equally to a term of Copyright at all. They were indeed chiefly those which were brought forward in the case of Millar against Taylor, and have been already discussed: such as the enhancing the price of books; the capricious refusal on the part of authors, or their representatives, to allow books to be printed, &c.

ness of young society have some interest about which affection may gather, and at least let them be protected from those who would exhibit them mangled or corrupted to their transatlantic disciples."

In moving the second reading of the Bill,* the learned Sergeant said, that he only wished the House at that stage of the Bill, to affirm the principle of it, which was, 'that the present term of Copyright was much too short for the attainment of that justice which society owes to authors, especially to those (few though they might be) whose reputation was of slow growth and of enduring character;' and he desired the House to recollect that all the other parts of the Bill were mere questions of detail.

In this speech he thus feelingly and justly alludes to the reward due to an author: "We cannot decide *the abstract question between genius and money,* because there exist no common properties by which they can be tested, if we were dispensing an arbitrary reward; but the question, how much the author ought to receive, is easily answered—so much as his readers are delighted to pay him. When we say that he has obtained immense wealth by his writings, what do we assert, but that he has multiplied the sources of enjoyment to countless readers, and lightened thousands of else sad, or weary, or dissolute hours? The two propositions are identical, the proof of the one at once establishing the other. Why then should we grudge it any more than we would reckon against the soldier, not the pension or the grant, but the very prize-money which attests the splendour of his victories, and in the amount of his gains proves the extent of ours? Complaints have been made by one in the foremost rank in the opposition to this bill, the pioneer of the noble army of publishers, booksellers, printers, and bookbinders, who are arrayed against it, that in selecting the case of Sir Walter Scott as an instance in which the extension of Copyright would be just, I had been singularly unfortunate, because that great writer received during the period of subsisting Copyright, an unprecedented revenue from the imme-

* On the 25th of April, 1838.

diate sale of his works. But, Sir, *the question is not one of reward—it is one of justice.* How would this gentleman approve of the application of a similar rule to his own honest gains? From small beginnings this very publisher has, in the fair and honourable course of trade I doubt not, acquired a splendid fortune, amassed by the sale of works the property of the public—of works whose authors have gone to their repose from the fevers, the disappointments, and the jealousies which await a life of literary toil. Who grudges it to him? Who doubts his title to retain it? And yet this gentleman's fortune is all, every farthing of it, so much taken from the public in the sense of the publisher's argument; it is all profit on books bought by that public, the accumulation of pence which, if he had sold his books without profit, would have remained in the pockets of the buyers. On what principle is Mr. Tegg to retain what is denied to Sir Walter? Is it the claim of superior merit? Is it greater toil? Is it larger public service? His course, I doubt not, has been that of an honest laborious tradesman; but what have been its anxieties, compared to the stupendous labour, the sharp agonies of him whose deadly alliance with those very trades whose members oppose me now, and whose noble resolution to combine the severest integrity with the loftiest genius, brought him to a premature grave—a grave which, by the operation of the law, extends its chillness even to the result of those labours, and despoils them of the living efficacy to assist those whom he has left to mourn him. Let any man contemplate that heroic struggle of which the affecting record has just been completed, and turn from the sad spectacle of one who had once rejoiced in the rapid creations of a thousand characters glowing from his brain, and stamped with individuality for ever, straining the fibres of the mind till the exercise which was delight became torture —girding himself to the mighty task of achieving his deliverance from the load which pressed upon him, and with brave endeavour, but relaxing strength, returning to the toil till his faculties give way, the pen falls from his hand on the unmarked paper, and the silent tears of half-conscious imbecility fall upon it—to some prosperous bookseller in his country-house, calculating the approach of the time (too swiftly accelerated) when he should be able to publish for his own gain, those works fatal to life; and then tell me, if we are to apportion the reward to the effort, where is the justice of the bookseller's claim? Had Sir Walter Scott been able to see in the distance an extension of his own right in his own productions, his estate and his heart had been set free; and the publishers and printers who are our opponents now, would have been grateful to him for a continuation of labour and rewards which would have impelled and augmented their own."

The learned Sergeant thus concluded a very able and eloquent speech: "True it is that in many instances, if the boon be granted, the errors and frailties which often attend genius may render it vain; true it is that in multitudes of cases it will not operate, but we shall have given to authors and to readers a great lesson of justice; we shall have shown that where genius and virtue combine we are ready to protect their noble offspring, and that we do not desire a miserable advantage at the cost of the ornaments and benefactors of the world. I call on each party in this house to unite in rendering this tribute to the minds by which even party associations are dignified; on those who anticipate successive changes in society, to acknowledge their debt to those who expand the vista of the future, and people it with goodly visions; on those who fondly linger on the past and repose on time-hallowed institutions, to consider how much that is ennobling in their creed has been drawn from minds which have clothed the usages and forms of other days with the symbols of venerableness and beauty; on all, if they cannot find some common ground on which they may unite in drawing assurance of progressive good for the future from the glories of the past, to recognize their obligation to those, the products of whose intellect shall grace, and soften, and dignify the struggle."

Mr. Hume then addressed the House against the Bill, but his arguments only amounted to this: that the effect of the Bill would be to enhance the price of books, and so limit the scope of intellectual enjoyment, and the advancement of useful learning; and this line of argument he conceived he fully proved by a statement that Sir Walter Scott's 'Lay of the last Minstrel,' first sold for two guineas, and could now be had for 1*s*. 6*d*.; and 'Marmion,' first sold at 1*l*. 8*s*. 6*d*., and could now be had for 10*d*.* The Solicitor General opposed the Bill, calling it 'a tax upon knowledge;' and used the ungenerous argument that 'because under the present system works were produced, it showed that somewhere there was a sufficient stimulus to exertion, and that for his part he would not consent to grant any further reward.' A long debate ensued, in the course of which Sir Robert Inglis, Mr. D'Israeli, Mr. Milne, the Chancellor of the Exchequer, Mr. Wynne, and Lord Mahon, spoke in favor of the second reading; Mr. Pryme, Mr. Ward, Mr. Grote, the Attorney General, † Mr. Jervis, Sir Edward Sugden, and Mr. Warburton opposed it.

The only argument of any seeming weight used by the opponents of this measure, was that publishers act like merchants, whose principle it always is to replace their capital with profit as soon as possible; that they do not care what is to take place 60 years hence, and that at the same time that they would seek to have an absolute assignment of the whole

* The utter inconsequence of these facts, so far as the construction sought to be drawn from them, must be obvious to any one of the least discrimination.

† The Attorney General suggested that the Bill should be altered into one to empower the judicial committee of the Privy Council to grant an extension of the present period of Copyright, under particular circumstances, the same as is now done with regard to patents.

term, they would not give the author any more for the 60 years extra than they would do under the existing state of law; and therefore the benefit of this Bill would be solely to the publishers. *

The house then divided, when there were Ayes, 39, Noes, 34, making a majority of five in favour of a second reading; and, upon another division, with a majority of seven in favour, the Bill was ordered to be committed.

On the 10th of May, on the motion that the house go into committee on the Bill, Mr. Wakley opposed it in a very humourous and amusing speech, but one that did not bear in any decided manner on the question. He entertained the House with a statement of the very small sums Mr. Tegg had given for various works, novels, romances, and on general subjects, which had been brought out at about 10s. a volume, and had been sold to Mr. Tegg from 8d. to a 1s.; generally within three or four years after publication: though what this was meant to prove, or what argument to support, it is impossible to say. Several other members spoke; and on the house dividing, there was a majority of 52 in favor of the motion out of 180 members present.

On the 6th of June, the House, after some discussion, went into a committee, pro formâ, to allow of some amendments being made to the Bill, one of which was, with respect to works already published, not to extend the further term of 60 years from the death of the author, to cases where the author had parted with his whole interest in the work under the existing law. And this was done on account of the opposition of the publishers to the reverting clause in such cases, on the grounds that in purchasing a Copyright they calculated upon having an equal right to print it with the

* But this argument defeats itself; for if the further term were worth nothing in the publisher's estimation, it is not to be supposed he would refuse to purchase, because the grant of it was denied: if, again, it seemed valuable, of course he would be willing to give an equivalent for it.

rest of the world at the end of the present existing term, from which they would be by this debarred. Indeed, as before stated, by the custom of the trade they enjoyed a practical prolongation of the term of Copyright which would have been thus taken away.

At this advanced stage of the Bill, Lord John Russell, who had not taken any part in the preceding debates, expressed his disapprobation of any measure at all on the subject. There was nothing new or that requires any notice in the speech of the noble Lord; he merely deprecated legislation on so difficult a question as Copyright, and required more time for the consideration of the Bill. Mr. Sergeant Talfourd, after observing that he scarcely expected the noble lord thus at the eleventh hour to start objections, not to the details, but to the principle of the Bill, named the 20th of June as a sufficiently distant day for the further consideration of the report. The Bill was then printed with the proposed amendments,* which, besides the one above referred to, consisted in alterations as to the mode of bringing an action or obtaining an injunction for piracy—a bonâ fide abridgment was not to be considered as such; alterations in the mode of giving notice in case of reprinting a work, not reprinted within five years after the author's death, and being out of print; as to the expunging entry in registry-book wrongfully or injuriously made; and as to the Copyright in encyclopædias and periodicals: and a clause was inserted to provide for the proof of Copyright in Colonial Courts, and another for saving all rights existing at the time of passing this act.

On the 20th of June, when the further consideration of the report was again brought forward, it was proposed that owing to the immense mass of public business before the House, the great division of opinion on its details, and the hopelessness of expecting that the Bill could be passed that session,

* This amended Bill was the one before the House this last session, (1839.)

the further consideration of the report should be put off for three months. To which Sergeant Talfourd acceded, observing that he did so with great reluctance, as it had arrived at so advanced a stage; but considering the extent of business, and the opposition which existed to some details, he did not think he should be sacrificing the interest of authors by acceding. The learned member observed, "The Bill has been remodelled, and when it appears in its amended form much of the present opposition to it will be removed. All the great publishers are favourable to it."

CHAPTER XIV.

THE INTERNATIONAL COPYRIGHT BILL, AND THE PROCEEDINGS ON SERGEANT TALFOURD'S BILL FOR THE AMENDMENT OF COPYRIGHT IN 1839.

In the meantime a Bill 'for securing to authors, in certain cases, the benefit of an international Copyright,' was brought before Parliament; and, meeting with little opposition, was passed, and received the royal assent on the 31st of July, 1838.* It empowers her Majesty, by Order in Council, to allow to foreigners Copyright in their works here, where the government to which those foreigners belong allow to British subjects printing in their dominions similar equivalent rights. There was a discussion in the House of Lords on the third reading, as to a proposed amendment requiring copies of works to be delivered to the Universities, besides the copy required by the Bill to be furnished to the British Museum. But on its being observed that if we exacted this from foreigners, foreign governments might, with equal justice, demand copies of our works, and thus, by an extended system of international Copyright throughout the continent, perhaps a hundred copies might be required, which would be so heavy a tax as to defeat the intentions of the act, the proposed amendment was not persisted in.

In the debate that had occurred on Sergeant Talfourd's Bill, on the 25th of April, 1838, the Attorney General had sug-

* 1 & 2 Vict. cap. 59.

gested that the Bill should be changed into one giving power to the judicial committee to extend the term of Copyright in certain cases, similar to the manner in which the terms of patents were usually extended. And in accordance with this suggestion, on the 27th of July, Lord Brougham brought a Bill to that effect into the House of Lords. This Bill got as far as the third reading, which being proposed for the 6th of August, the Marquess of Lansdowne said 'he was not aware it had proceeded so far, and hoped it would be allowed to stand over for a day or two, in order that their lordships might make themselves acquainted with its details,' which was acceded to. It was put off from day to day till the 9th, after which day no further mention of it was made, owing to the impracticability of passing it that session.

Early in the last year (1839) Sergeant Talfourd, unwearied and persevering, again brought in a Bill to amend the Law of Copyright; and moved the second reading of it, on the 27th of February, in a speech, like the preceding, able, eloquent, and convincing.

It had been objected by some of the opponents, on former occasions, that there were no petitions from authors, seeking for a further extension of their Copyright; and that it was strange to ask for them a boon, which they had not sought themselves. This objection the learned Sergeant now removed, by presenting several petitions from authors to that effect; and in reference to it, he observed: "When I first solicited for those arguments the notice of this House, I thought they rested on principles so general, that the interests of those who labour to instruct and illustrate the age in which they live are so inseparably blended with all that affects its morality and its happiness, that the due reward of the greatest of its authors is so identified with the impulses they quicken—with the traits of character they mirror—with the deeds of generosity, of courage, and of virtue which they celebrate, and with the multitudes whom they delight and refine, that I felt it was not for them alone that I asked the shelter of the law, and I did not wish to see them soliciting it as a personal boon."

Respecting the fears of the printers that if Copyright were extended, books would be dearer, fewer would be printed, fewer hands would be required, fewer presses set up, fewer types cast, fewer reams of paper needed, the learned Sergeant observes: "Now, if there were any real ground for those busy fears, they would not want facts to support them. In the year 1814, when the term of Copyright was extended from fourteen to twenty-eight years, the same class expressed similar alarms. The projected change was far more likely to be prejudicial to them than the present, as the number of books on which it operated was much larger; and yet there is no suggestion in their petitions, that a single press remained unemployed, or a paper-mill stood still; and, indeed, it is matter of notoriety, that since then, publications have greatly multiplied, and that books have been reduced in price with the increase of readers."

After alluding to the petitions from authors, he says: "Now, I ask, is there no property in these petitioners worthy of protection? 'No,' said, and will say, some of the opponents of this Bill; 'none. We think that from the moment an author puts his thoughts on paper, and delivers them to the world, his property therein wholly ceases.' What! has he invested no capital? embarked no fortune? *If human life is nothing in your commercial tables—if the sacrifice of profession, of health, of gain is nothing, surely the mere outlay of him who has perilled his fortune to instruct mankind, may claim some regard!* Or is the interest itself so refined—so ethereal—that you cannot regard it as property, because it is not palpable to sense or to feeling? Is there any justice in this? If so, why do you protect moral character as a man's most precious possession, and compensate the party who suffers in that character unjustly by damages? Has this possession any existence half so palpable as the author's right in the printed creation of his brain? I have always thought it one of the proudest triumphs of human law that it is able to recognize and to guard this breath and finer spirit of moral action—that it can lend its aid in sheltering that invisible property which exists solely in the action and affection of others, and, if it may do this, why may it not protect him in his right—those words which, as well observed by a great thinker, are, 'after all, the only things that last for ever?'"

As to the enhancing the price of books:—"But grant the whole *assumption*—grant that if Copyright be extended, the few books it will affect will be dearer to the public by the little the author will gain by each copy—grant that they will not be more correct or authentic than when issued wholesale from the press; still is there nothing good for the people but cheap knowledge? Is it necessary to associate with their introduction to the works of the mighty dead, the selfish thought that they are sharing in the riot of the grave, instead of cherishing a sense of pride that, while they read, they are assisting to deprive the grave of some of its withering power over the interests of survivors? But if it were desirable, is it possible to separate a personal sympathy with an author from the young admiration of his works? We do not enter into his labours, as into some strange and dreamy world, raised by the touch of a forgotten enchanter; the affections are breathing around us, and the author being dead, yet speaks in accents triumphant over death and time. As from the dead level of an utilitarian philosophy no mighty work of genius ever issues, so never can such a work be enjoyed except in happy forgetfulness of its doctrines, which always softens the harshest creed. But I believe that those who thus plead for the people, are wholly unauthorized by their feelings; that the poor of these realms are richer in spirit than as their advocates understand them; and that they would feel a pride in bestowing their contributions in the expression of respect to that great intellectual ancestry, whose fame is as much theirs as it is the boast of the loftiest amongst us."

The learned Sergeant thus concluded: "I have been accused of asking you to legislate 'on some sort of sentimental feeling.' I deny the charge; the living truth is with us, the spectral phantoms of depopulated printing-houses and shops are with our opponents. If I were here beseeching indulgence for the frailties and excesses which sometimes attend fine talents — if I were appealing to your sympathy on behalf of crushed hopes and irregular aspirations, I might justly thus be charged. Not for the wild, but for the sage; not for the perishing, but for the eternal; for him who, poet, philosopher, or historian, girds himself for some toil lasting as life—lays aside all frivolous pursuits for one virtuous purpose, that when encouraged by that 'All hail hereafter,' which shall welcome him among the heirs of fame, he may not shudder to think of it as sounding with hollow mockery in the ears of those whom he loves, and waking sullen echoes by the side of a cheerless hearthstone: for such I ask this boon, and through them for mankind; and I ask it in the confidence with the expression of which your veteran petitioner, Wordsworth, closes his appeal to you,—'*That in this, as in all other cases, justice is capable of working out its own expediency.*'"

Some debate then ensued: Mr. O'Connell, Sir Robert Inglis, and the Chancellor of the Exchequer, supported the second reading; Mr. Hume, Mr. Warburton, Mr. Baines, and the Solicitor General, opposed it. No new arguments were used against the bill except this: Mr. Warburton remarked that under this act, "It would be impossible to republish old works without a tedious, expensive, and troublesome process, including an application to the Court of Chancery, to say nothing of its imposing upon publishers an obligation from which persons in other trades were exempt; that of giving public notice of the speculations in which they were about to engage; and that would surely be hardly fair when other persons in business were allowed to keep their operations secret." He also urged that in works requiring a considerable time, and where expense must likewise be encountered, it was likely that authors would receive advances, and part with their works to the publishers altogether.—"The object of the author, as of the publisher, is to obtain immediate advances; and is it possible, by any arrangements we can make under this Bill, to prevent authors, first from receiving their advances, and then parting with the work altogether? Is the author likely, in that case, to make a much better bargain than he does at present? By no means. While, by his doing so he, or rather the legislature which permits it, will be depriving the public of what they are fairly entitled to, and to which they certainly have a stronger claim than the publisher, to whom the additional pecuniary benefit, should any arise, must fall." The Solicitor General reiterated in more unequivocal terms his design to reduce authors to what was not inappropriately termed by another member, 'a work-house allowance.' "My own opinion," said the learned gentleman, "is that books should be had for the benefit of the public at the lowest possible prices; and therefore *no greater inducement should be held out to authors* than may be necessary for securing the production of the desired works. I can never bring myself to support any measure which goes farther than to give authors *the minimum* of inducement to produce their works."

The House divided, when there was a majority of 36 out of 110 members present in favour of the second reading; and the Bill was committed for Wednesday the 10th of April.

It was put off from day to day till Wednesday the 1st of May, when on the question that the House should go into Committee on the Bill, a most vexatious and unusual course of opposition was taken. Messrs. Warburton and Wakley, and a few others, persisted in repeatedly moving adjournments; and although considerable indignation was manifested by a large majority of the House at this unwonted exercise of a proper privilege which the minority have to prevent surprise; they divided the House, with decreasing numbers, no less than twenty times, and so far gained their object, that little progress was made with the Bill, the four first clauses only being agreed to. The pretext for this conduct was, the Bill being brought forward on a Wednesday night; although it was impossible to get any other night, from the state of the public business.

As the same conduct was again threatened unless the Bill was brought forward on some other night in the week, which could not be done, it was put off from day to day till the 8th of July, when Sergeant Talfourd, on the order of the day being read for the House to go into Committee on the Bill, said that 'considering the opposition with which the Bill was threatened, and the state of the public business at this late period of the session, however anxious he and the party with whom he acted, were to proceed with it, they could not entertain any reasonable hope of carrying the Bill through the House of Commons at such a period, and asking the House of Lords to proceed to legislate on it.' He therefore would not occupy the time of the House any further with it at this time, but 'he should be ready to renew his struggle with the honourable member for Bridport at the earliest possible period of the next session.'

CHAPTER XV.

OBSERVATIONS ON SERGEANT TALFOURD'S BILL.

Having in this slight sketch brought down the history of Copyright to the present period; having traced its recognition from the earliest time when such a property could exist, in the exclusive privileges, decrees of Star Chamber, ordinances and Acts of Parliament, usages and by-laws of the Stationers' Company, and in the universal and unrefuted opinion entertained at the time of passing the 8 Anne, c. 19, and solemnly and legally confirmed by the decision of the Court of King's Bench in the case of Millar against Taylor; having shown that the statute of Anne is not to be held as abrogating that common-law right, and that the subsequent judgment of the House of Peers, reversing the decision of the King's Bench, is not to be considered as a sound construction; having detailed all the measures that have been subsequently adopted, either in diminution or increase of the interest of an author in his copy, down to the present moment, it remains for us to notice the objections which have been urged against the plan now proposed by Mr. Sergeant Talfourd.

The arguments against Sergeant Talfourd's Bill are: that the proposed extension of term will be profitless to the author, indifferent to the publisher, and injurious to the public. It will be profitless to the author, because it will affect only one case out of five hundred; and in that one case the author will most likely have parted with his whole interest to the bookseller. It will be indifferent to the publisher, for he will make his calculations either with or without reference to the future term; and either way, on the principles on which his present trade is conducted, will only have to blame his own want of foresight or fortune. And it will be injurious to the public, because the only works that it will affect, will be those which it is most desirable should be circulated in a cheap form; namely, works of sterling merit, which outlive the ephemeral productions of the day, and by the perusal of which, mankind become wiser and more useful members of society.

But these arguments, however specious they may seem, are futile. For although it were granted that the proposed extension would affect only one case out of five hundred; if such be the proportion of works of real merit to the number of trifling performances, it is all that is sought to be obtained. For the object of the Bill is not to give a greater value to the light and trivial productions of the day, which either reap a sufficient and quick reward from their admirers, or fall with well merited contempt into oblivion; but to secure to authors of genius and learning—whose works, although they become the classics of the country, often make their way but slowly into public favour—some slight pecuniary advantage, by extending their Copyright for a further period, at the very time it has commenced to be valuable, and to repay them for their long and unceasing labours. And although such cases are by their very nature rare, their infrequency forms no reason for treating them with neglect. And it is no sound argument against the extension, were it even the case, that the author may have assigned away his whole interest in his works; for such a line of reasoning would equally have applied in 1814, to the extension to 28 years certain of the term of Copyright. But experience has shown that it is not by any means an unusual practice for authors, even under the present law, to dispose of their works for an edition only, or for a certain term of years, with an interest reverting back to themselves. And indeed the opponents of this Bill use an argument that contradicts itself, when they assert that a bookseller will regard the future term as not worth buying, and therefore will give no more for the extended term than he does at present; and yet, with the same breath, say, that he will insist on having what is thus, according to them, an utterly valueless privilege.

Then as to the objection that it will injure the public. The public can have no right to demand that any one should dedicate his life *gratuitously* to their service. Therefore authors ought to have a reward, and the only question is as to its amount; whether the reward that shall be given to those who instruct, shall be less than to those who amuse mankind: whether we shall caress and enrich the contributors to the pleasure of the moment, and neglect and deprive of their just property, those who dedicate themselves to enlighten not only the present race, but posterity. For such is the state of the present law. Man is slow to acknowledge reason, and inattentive to the voice of wisdom; and when at last he does bow to their precepts, and admit their force, he at the same time proclaims that the reward so long withheld shall not continue; but, in most instances, cease almost with its first existence. What must be the effect of such conduct as this, but to make authors fall in with the follies and humours of the age; and as the future offers them no reward, look only to the approbation of the present?

But grant even, with Lord Camden, that genius for itself would spurn every sordid consideration that should interfere with its flight, or deaden the elastic energy of its pinion; yet could it, or ought it, to disregard those links that attach it to the earth? Has an author no social ties? Has he no children who look to him for their advancement; no wife who clings to him for support? Is he to take upon himself the heavy moral responsibility of neglecting their interests for what, he may at moments accuse himself, is after all but a craving for vain glory? Is he to devote his whole energies, his talents, his life; is he to experience the misgivings, the unceasing mental anxiety, the intellectual toil; is he to put aside pleasure, interest, and passion, and apply himself through sickness and pain, through fast and vigil, through the sleepless night and the care-worn day, to the composition of a work which shall delight and instruct his own and future ages, for an unthankful and ungracious public, who, whilst they greedily snatch at the fruit of his labours, refuse grudgingly the small recompence which might rescue himself or his children from poverty and misery?

But it is far from clear that this injury to the public, which it is said the extension of Copyright will occasion, is not an ideal one. For it is only founded on the supposition that books will be made dearer by the change, which, at the best, is but problematical. At all events, the difference in price will be but trifling; for now that within late years the class of readers has become so increased, it is the publisher's object to sell his books at the cheapest possible rate; it being a recently yet universally recognized maxim in trade, that a large sale and a low profit are better than a limited sale and a high one. Therefore all that the public will have to give more for a book, under an extended period of Copyright, than they do at present, will be the proportion of the sum paid to the author for the Copyright.* And accordingly, as the book is more valuable and useful to the public, they will have to pay less for it; since a greater number of copies can be printed at once, and a less sum charged on each, will remunerate the author. So that whilst this bill will not affect the ordinary run of works at all, it will afford protection to works

* I find I am fully borne out in this view, by the statements made by an eminent American bookseller, who has published some very excellent remarks on the subject,—Mr. Nicklin of Philadelphia; although I am sorry to find he is, like most Americans, opposed to a system of international copyright, at least as far as regards the reprinting in the United States the works of British authors.

of real merit and worth, and, in proportion to their merit and to the desire of the public for their perusal, they will cost the public less and reward the author more.

The arguments brought forward by the opponents of the bill, on this subject, obviously contradict one another. With one breath they urge against this measure, that no works will be benefited by it; with the next, they draw a moving picture of the evils that will ensue from it, by enhancing the price of books.* As this line of reasoning is contradictory, so is that inconsequent, in which it is attempted to draw an inference, from the difference of the price of certain books now, from what they were first published at, that it is the effect of Copyright to keep books at excessive prices. For it must be apparent to every one, that as the number of readers has greatly increased of late years, the practice of cheap editions has become more universal; and that the moderate price at which they are now sold, is owing principally to the greater demand for them, and the lessened expenses of large editions.

But, important as it is that the public should have good and useful works at a moderate price, it is equally so that they should have them correct and free from error. And how does the present law bear upon this point? Most injuriously; for an author may considerably alter and amend his

* Mr. Tegg, a great opponent of this measure, has these remarkably inconsistent statements in his petition to the House. He says, "most of the scenes about, and subjects on which, books are written, are in the course of continual change, so that *extension of Copyright would be of no service to authors in general*; for *none would benefit by it*, but those whose works are of an unchangeable character — such as *chiefly poets and novelists*." And then submits to the House, "that the national advantages of literature to the country, by facilitating *instruction*, supplying *historical and scientific* information, inculcating *just, honourable, and religious principles*, and affording a refined species of entertainment, would be counteracted, and the *immense efforts to extend education* partially *frustrated*, by the measures proposed by Sergeant Talfourd." Appendix to Seventh Report on Public Petitions. (27th Feb.—1st March, 1839.) No. 187.

Did it never occur to this gentleman, that he could not at the same time as-work by after experience; and when he does, the Copyright may have expired in his unamended and first edition, but not in the one that has had the benefit of his more mature wisdom, and the first be issued again to the world with all its faults and errors; which could not be the case, if the Copyright in the work still remained for some period after the author's decease.

Therefore, inasmuch as an extension of Copyright could only confer a reward upon those whose works richly deserve it; as it would be a reward conferred solely by the free-will of the public; as it could not affect works of transient or temporary interest, neither raising nor lowering their price, but only those of standard and sterling merit; as it would be difficult in any other manner to reward literary effort so well and justly as by making it wholly dependent on the voluntary contributions of the public; as by the existing law, the remuneration for standard works of history, religion, and science is notoriously inadequate compared with the sums given for light and trifling pieces, which please for the moment; and as any measure which should make the author dependent on the pleasure of a particular tribunal for a further reward, would be an insufficient, unsatisfactory, and unjust mode of proceeding, since none can set a price upon talent, or estimate, by commercial or mathematical scales, the exact value of intellectual exertion;—for one and all of these reasons, it is to be hoped that the principle of Sergeant Talfourd's bill may be passed, and England will no longer be to be reproached as the tardiest of nations in according justice to authors.†

sume that this bill would only affect "poets and novelists," and yet trace to its wide influence all the above evils? That he could not at one moment censure it as benefiting few authors, and therefore applying to few works, and the next, as applying to all works, and therefore injuring the public?

† The term of Copyright is greater in almost every other country than in England. See the Appendix.

I say, the principle, because it is not at all clear that the extension of the Copyright should be to exactly sixty years from the death of the author; indeed, as a matter of opinion, I am almost inclined to think that two-thirds of that period, or perhaps even less, would be sufficient.

Besides, there are some of the details of the bill that might be altered, and no doubt will be, before it is passed into a law; such, for instance, as the anomaly which has been objected to it, with regard to works already published, of giving to an author who has retained the whole, or a portion of the interest in his own hands, the benefit of the extension of the term; but denying it in the case of another, who, not having the same means or good fortune, has assigned away all his interest. There is no other reason for this distinction, but because in such cases, the assignee cannot claim the future term, for which he has paid nothing; and it cannot be given to the author, for it would be unjust to the assignee, since the assignee, in making his bargain with the author, calculated with reference to the present law, that he should have the same right, at the expiration of his term, to print it, as the rest of the world, and a greater, practically, by the custom of the trade amongst booksellers; and therefore it would not be fair to compel him, either to pay for the future term, or forego the advantages he would otherwise have had when his Copyright expired, in publishing the work under the present law. But what objection can there exist to a clause being framed, giving the author or his heirs, in such cases, a power to assign the future interest *only to one party*, namely, to the assignee of the original term? In the case of a work of merit, the interest in which has been wholly assigned, the publisher to whom it is assigned would be very willing to purchase the extended period on terms very advantageous to the author; and it would be hard, under such circumstances, where it could injure no one, that the author should be deprived of the benefit, merely because he had not retained a share of the interest in his own hands. And where the author and the assignee could not agree upon terms, and no such future assignment was made, then the Copyright should expire, as it would otherwise do, under the present existing law. Those who are captious enough to take extreme objections, may urge that a case might arise, where a bookseller might capriciously refuse to purchase, except at terms extremely disadvantageous to the author; and thus the author would be left wholly at his mercy. But those who would urge this, forget altogether, that without such a clause, no author at all, who has assigned away the whole of his interest, can receive any benefit by the bill as it now stands.

And again, a clause, allowing parties to print a book when out of print for five years, on advertising publicly their intention so to do, and suffering a year from the date thereof to elapse, is much objected to, on account of the difficulties it is supposed in practice it would present; but it might perhaps be altered into a clause to the same effect, without the same inconveniences. For instance, if proof of demand made at the house of the publishers of the last edition, once every year, for three, four, or five successive years, with the same answer, that it was out of print, (or any other proof of a similar nature, that the work had been out of print for four or five years,) should be held to be a *primâ facie* case, to entitle a party to reprint it, and throw the onus of showing that he was aware that it was not out of print, or that a new edition was preparing, on the author or his assignee. Such a clause would protect the owner of Copyright; at the same time it would not check enterprize, by obliging publicity to be given to a speculation of a purely mercantile nature, and thus awakening competition. It is absurd to contend, as has been done, that a publisher, not wishing to reprint himself, nor that others should reprint, might keep some copies by him to show that it was not out of print; for if the work was worth reprinting, a sale would be found for these remaining copies, and he could not refuse to sell.

The foregoing objections are entirely to matters of detail, which may be easily remedied, and do not in any way interfere with the main principle of the bill.

Therefore we doubt not that a measure, so imperatively one of national justice; which has for its object the benefit of the good and the great, and tends to make the reward of merit proportionally greater than that of fortune; which allows genius and learning to pursue their labours in the face of death, secure in the knowledge that the fame which posterity will confer on their name, will not be unaccompanied by substantial benefits to their family, and that they have not to blame themselves for pursuing an empty vanity, and neglecting the provision of a competence for those they leave to bewail their loss; but have obtained the one by the same efforts as the other, and fulfilled at the same time their aspirations for fame and their duties as members of society—will receive the unqualified sanction of the legislature—and we shall then at least have done something to avoid that eloquent reproach of Dryden,—"that it continues to be the ingratitude of mankind, that they who teach wisdom by the surest means, shall generally live poor and unregarded, as if they were born only for the public, and had no interest in their own well-being, but were to be lighted up like tapers, and waste themselves for the benefit of others."

APPENDIX,

CONTAINING

THE STATE OF COPYRIGHT IN FOREIGN COUNTRIES.

"C'est surtout par la législation comparée que la question de propriété littéraire peut avancer vers sa solution; car c'est en combinant les systèmes adoptés par des peuples aussi divers par leurs institutions que par leurs mœurs, qu'on reconnaîtra quelle est sa véritable essence et jusqu'à quel point elle peut se constituer par elle-même, sans le secours de l'autorité civile, ou bien si effectivement les droits de chacun sur l'œuvre livrée à tous, ne peuvent se trouver réglés que par la puissance publique."

M. Victor Foucher.

LIST OF COUNTRIES,

A NOTICE OF THE LAW OF COPYRIGHT IN WHICH IS CONTAINED IN THE APPENDIX.

AMERICA.

FRANCE.

HOLLAND AND BELGIUM.

States of the GERMANIC CONFEDERATION, Collectively.

Separately I. Austria.

——— II. Prussia.

——— III. Bavaria.

——— IV. Wurtemberg.

——— V. Baden.

——— VI. Hesse Cassel.

——— VII. Saxe Coburg Gotha.

——— VIII. Saxe Meiningen.

——— IX. Hamburgh.

——— X. Other States.

RUSSIA.

DENMARK.

NORWAY AND SWEDEN.

SPAIN.

THE TWO SICILIES.

APPENDIX.

THE UNITED STATES.

Before the separation of the American colonies from the mother country, a Law of Copyright there was equally unnecessary and unknown. But the intellectual activity which the struggle for their independence created, and their success increased, soon called for some protection of its labours; and different laws were passed for this purpose by the legislatures of the several States. But as no effectual remedy could be had by these means, since the work protected in one State might be re-printed immediately in the adjoining one, it was made one of the articles in the Constitution of the United States that Congress should have power, "to promote the progress of science and the useful arts, by securing for limited times, to authors and inventors the exclusive right to their respective writings and discoveries." *

In pursuance of this power, Congress as early as the second session, 1790, passed an act framed on the model of the 8 Anne, c. 19, by which an absolute term of 14 years was given to the author, with a contingency of another 14 years, should he survive the first 14. † This was amended by a subsequent act, ‡ in 1802; but they are now both repealed by an act passed the 3rd of Feb. 1831, || which is the existing regulation on the subject.

By this act, the Copyright in a work is secured to an author being a citizen of the United States, or resident therein, *for the term of 28 years;* and if either he, his wife, or children, survive that period,

* Sec. 8. Story on Const. of U. S. vol. 3. p. 48.

† Passed May 31, 1790. ‡ April 29, 1802.

|| Gordon's Dig. of Amer. Laws. A supplementary law to this was passed in 1834, respecting certain formalities to be observed in assigning Copyright.

then *for a further term of* 14 *years.* * The proceedings necessary to be taken to secure the Copyright, &c., are also much simplified and amended.

The penalty for piracy, besides the confiscation of the pirated edition for the use of the party aggrieved, is fifty cents for every sheet found in the possession of the offender.

The report of the Judiciary Committee, on which the above act was founded, was couched in terms which would have led one to expect a greater boon to authors, than it affords. They say:—

"Your committee believe that the just claims of authors require from our legislation, a protection not less than what is proposed in the Bill reported. Upon the first principles of proprietorship in property, an author has an exclusive and *perpetual* right, in preference to any other, to the fruits of his labour. Though the nature of literary property is peculiar, it is not the less real and valuable. If labour and effort in producing what before was not possessed or known will give title, then the literary man has title, perfect and absolute, and should have his reward: he writes and he labours as assiduously as does the mechanic or husbandman. The scholar who secludes himself, and wastes his life, and often his property to enlighten the world, has the best right to the profits of those labours: the planter, the mechanic, the professional man cannot prefer a better title to what is admitted to be his own. Nor is there any doubt what the interest and honour of the country demand on this subject. We are justly proud of the knowledge and virtue of our fellow-citizens. Shall we not encourage the means of that knowledge, and enlighten that virtue, so necessary to the security and judicious exercise of civil and political rights? We ought to present every reasonable inducement to influence men to consecrate their talents to the advancement of science. It cannot be for the interest or honour of our country that intellectual labour should be depreciated, and a life devoted to research and laborious study terminate in disappointment and poverty." †

A legal American writer of some repute, ‡ thus accounts for the difference between the Bill reported and the language of the report:

"It will be seen," says he, "by the above extract, that a respectable committee of the House of Representatives assert, that an author, according to all the

* "Whether this contingent term be assignable before the expiration of the first term, seems uncertain." Nicklin on Lit. Prop. p. 76.

† In the Amer. Jurist. vol. x, p. 79, 80.

‡ The writer of the article on Lit. Prop. in the Amer. Jurist. vol. x, is so spoken of by Mr. Nicklin, p. 68.

rules of law, has a perpetual Copyright; and it is evident that that committee would have reported a Bill to this effect, if they had thought the *public mind prepared* for so great a change *at one stride*. But *the time*, we venture to augur, *is not far distant* when authors will be placed upon an equality with their fellow men in the enjoyment of what they earn by their labour. The public are growing more and more disposed to admit, that if there be one description of property which merits more protection, or one which it is more politic to favour than another, it is literary property; and certainly if there be any sum which the public are more free in paying than another, it is the trivial extra sum put upon a book, which is intended for the author's pocket."

On the 16th of Feb. 1837, a report was made, and a Bill subsequently brought in, to extend to authors of Great Britain the same privileges as American authors enjoyed; but I do not find that anything was done to follow up these steps. The report was brought in by Mr. Clay, and from the liberality and justness of its sentiments, does honour to its framers: but it is a difficult task to persuade a nation to forego a benefit, merely because it is just to do so; and America will ever be unwilling to extend to British authors a protection, while she cannot claim from Great Britain an equivalent advantage, having comparatively few or no authors to profit by a similar protection to American authors in England.

In the meantime, however, an amendment of the law of 1831, by a further extension of the term of Copyright, is much talked of in America.

FRANCE.

In France, as in England, the first protection that literary property received, was by means of privileges: but with this difference, that the infringement of those privileges in the former country, was visited with much heavier penalties, than in the latter. For the printing a work, the sole right to which belonged to another, was looked on as little better than theft, and punished accordingly. Indeed, it was said, that such conduct was worse than to enter a neighbour's house and steal his goods: for negligence might be imputed to him for permitting the thief to enter: but in the case of piracy of Copyright, it was stealing a thing confided to the public honour.

And in this light did Louis XIV. treat it, when he issued an edict dated the 27th of February, 1682, by which he prohibited all booksellers and printers of Lyons, and others, from printing any books, the sole privilege of printing which, had been granted to another; on pain of corporal punishment.

The severity of this law, was somewhat softened by a subsequent edict of August, 1686; according to which, the penalty of corporal punishment was only incurred by a second offence: but the party so offending twice, was for ever disabled from exercising his trade of bookseller or printer.

These injunctions were renewed by an order of the 28th of February, 1723, Art. 109: but notwithstanding, piracies of books so much increased, that it was found necessary to put some heavier penalties on parties offending. An edict of council was accordingly passed,* by which all printers printing a pirated book, and all booksellers in whose possession copies of such pirated edition should be found; were liable, each, to a penalty of 6,000 *livres*: and for a second offence in addition to the above fine, were rendered incapable of ever again exercising their respective trades. Besides this, they were held liable in a demand for damages, at the suit of the parties injured; and by a subsequent edict,† this demand might be enforced by bill and information.

The protection that these edicts afforded to literary property, was, however, taken away by the famous decree of the National Assembly, by which all *privileges* of whatever kind they might be, were abolished.‡ But as amidst the tumult and confusion that attended

† 30th August, 1777. There were two edicts of the same date. Mr. Okey, the counsel to the British Embassy at Paris, in a communication obligingly furnished to the author, thus states the effect of the other:—" By a decree of the Council in 1777, (under Louis XVI.) when a privilege was granted to the author of a work, it was vested in him and his heirs for ever, until he assigned it. Upon assignment, the privilege lasted only during the life of the author. When leave to print, was granted to booksellers or printers, it could not be for less than ten years; and held good, during the life of the author, if he survived that period, or any other period fixed: the privilege could be renewed, when the work was increased by one fourth.

* 30th July, 1778.

‡ 4th of August, 1789.

the civil wars in England, this property was not long suffered to remained unprotected: so even amidst the horrors of the French revolution, measures to secure and preserve the rights of authors were not neglected. A decree was passed on the 19th of July, 1793, by which it was declared, that authors should enjoy exclusively, during their lives, the emoluments of their works; and that their heirs or assigns, should enjoy the same, for the term of ten years after their death, on penalty of a fine equivalent in value to three thousand copies of the original edition.*

It is, as Chancellor Kent well remarks,† 'A singular fact in the history of mankind, that the French National Convention in 1793, should have busied themselves with a law of this kind, when the whole Republic was at that time in the most violent convulsions; when the combined armies were invading France, and besieging Valenciennes; and when Paris was one scene of sedition, terror, proscription, imprisonment, and judicial massacre.'

The next law that was passed on the subject, and which is the one now in force, is a government decree under the empire, dated the 5th of February, 1810; by which the property in a work, is secured to the author *for his life*, to his widow *for her life*, and *after their death*, to their children *for twenty years*.‡ And besides an action for damages given to the author and his assigns, and the copies confiscated for his profit, a penalty is imposed of not more than 2,000 or less than 100 fr. against the party offending.‖

This law is, however, far from being considered satisfactory; both on account of the shortness of the term of Copyright

* This decree was introduced by Lakanal, who in making the report, thus ostentatiously described literary property. " De toutes les propriétés, la moins susceptible de contestation, c'est, sans contredit, celle des productions du génie; et, si quelque chose peut étonner, c'est qu'il ait fallu reconnaître cette propriété, assurer son libre exercice par une loi positive; c'est qu'une aussi grande révolution que la nôtre ait été nécessaire pour nous ramener sur ce point, comme sur tant d'autres, aux simples éléments de la justice la plus commune."

† 2 Kent's Comm. 378.

‡ Art. 39 and 40. " If there are no children," says M. Victor Foucher, Rev. Etr. de legisl. tom iv. p. 338, " then the other heirs or assignees, only enjoy the exclusive privilege for a period of ten years from the death of the author."

‖ Code pénal, 1810, Art. 427.

in particular cases, and of a distinction created by it, between dramatic and other writers. A commission was appointed as early as in 1825, with M. le vicomte de la Rochefoucauld at its head, to examine into, and remedy these evils. They submitted a project, by which the term of Copyright was to extend to fifty years from the death of the author, for the benefit of his widow, his heirs, legatees, or donees ; and in case of posthumous works, for a period of fifty years to the proprietor of the same. And if the author in his life-time should have assigned away his interest to a third party ; that then such party, should pay by consent, or by force of law,* a further sum to his heirs, by way of compensation.

This report was only agreed on, after numerous meetings, and long and grave deliberations ; and from the high scientific and literary character of those who assisted at its discussions, seemed to merit both attention and success. However, no steps appear to have been taken in consequence of their recommendation.

In 1837, a commission was again appointed, under the presidency of M. le comte de Ségur, to determine the nature of the rights of authors, and to fix their duration ; and they came to a resolution in the same spirit with that of 1825 :—that the existing regulations should still be preserved, but that the term after the author's death should be for fifty years, to the widow and representatives of the author.

In this report, the noble president says, that

'The commission had no difficulty in deciding that published works of art, of science, or of letters, ought to be considered as absolute property, of which the author has the right to preserve the entire disposal; and that this property is transmissible with the same rights, in the hands of his heirs or assigns ; at the same time acknowledging that after the death of the author, the right of property in his heir undergoes a modification : that it is mixed up with the right which society has acquired to its publication, a right, which the heir of the author has no longer the power to deny them.'

A commission was also charged, in 1837, to consider the state of Copyright as respects the works of French authors reprinted abroad ;

* " payer à l'aimable, ou judiciairement."

and in the report they presented,* they recommend the following articles ;—

1st. That as any measure having for its object the protection of French Copyrights abroad, must offer to foreigners the same security for their Copyrights in France, the following provisions shall be passed :—

That no works, published for the first time in a foreign country, shall be reprinted in France either during the life of the author, or for a certain period after his death, to be fixed by treaty, without the consent of the author or his representative ; and that every work so printed shall be reputed a piracy, and subject to all its penalties.

That this provision shall apply only to the works of those countries, in which a similar protection shall be afforded to French works first published in France.

And that no books printed abroad in the French tongue, shall be permitted to be imported into France, except at certain frontier towns therein named, unless such as are clearly for the personal use of the possessor.

These provisions were chiefly aimed at Belgium, from whose capital all Europe is supplied with the best productions of French literature at half the price of the French editions; but unluckily for the authors of France, Belgium is little likely to enter into any reciprocal treaty on the subject, for she does not hesitate to assign to France, as a reason for her refusal, as America has assigned to England, that she would thus be depriving herself of a lucrative branch of trade, without having any authors to reap a consequent advantage by the protection of their Copyrights in France.

In the beginning of last year, 1839, a Bill was introduced into the French legislature, by M. de Salvandy, (most probably originating from the report of M. le Comte de Ségur above noticed), having for its object the prolongation of the term of Copyright to 30 years after the death of the author; but in the angry and tumultuous debates which that short session produced, the Bill was lost sight of, and subsequently abandoned.

In the King's speech, on opening the Chambers this year, (January 1840), allusion is made to a projected measure for the amendment of the law of literary property ; but I am informed that this refers more particularly to the state of international law between France and Belgium, and not to any intention of lengthening the present term of Copyright.

* Printed in the '*Moniteur*' of 20 Feb. 1837.

In the meantime, however, several pamphlets have appeared on the subject, strongly advocating an alteration, and forcibly exposing the injustice of the present law in some instances. In one of these, the author, Mons. Bossange, an eminent French bookseller, even goes the length of advocating the principle of perpetuity. He says :—

"La justice, le bon sens, et l'équité, veulent que la propriété littéraire ne soit plus un mensonge sous forme de concession temporaire. Il faut qu'elle soit une propriété garantie par les lois, *inviolable et toujours.*"

The same writer also proposes the adoption of a new species of Copyright, which is not unworthy of consideration. After a certain period, according to his scheme, every work shall be open to any to print, on payment of a certain fixed sum to the proprietor of the Copyright, (which shall be perpetual) according to the number of copies sought to be printed.

HOLLAND AND BELGIUM.

When Belgium ceased, in 1814, to be a portion of the French Empire, a decree was issued* repealing all the French laws on printing and books, and enacting that in future, the author of every original work should have the exclusive right of printing and selling it, throughout the government of Belgium, during the life of the author, and his widow and heirs, after his death, for their respective lives. And any one importing or printing the same without the consent of such parties, during the above periods, should forfeit all the copies and a sum equivalent in value to three hundred copies of the original edition, both for the use of the party aggrieved; excepting always that a single copy of a work which a person might bring for his own use into Belgium, should not subject such person to the fine, but only to the confiscation of the copy.

Not long afterwards a law was passed,† which being made for the whole kingdom of the Netherlands, embraced likewise Belgium, and repealed the foregoing decree wherever the enactments contained were contradictory.

* 23 Sept. 1814. † 25 Jan. 1817.

It limits the duration of Copyright to the author *for his life*, and to his heirs or representatives, *for twenty years after his death*, on penalty of confiscation of all the unsold pirated copies in the kingdom to the use of the proprietor of the Copyright; of a fine equivalent in value to 2000 copies of the original edition, also to the use of the proprietor; besides a fine of not more than a thousand, nor less than an hundred florins, to be given to the poor of the district where the offender resides; and in case of a second offence, the offender to be disabled from the exercise of his trade of printer or bookseller, the whole without prejudice to the provisions and penalties, imposed or to be imposed by the general laws respecting piratical printing.

Although Holland and Belgium are now separate kingdoms, I understand this law is the one still in force in both countries. It has been styled the Act of *habeas animam*, on account of the protection which its accumulation of penalties confers on the productions of authors in those countries.

GERMANY.

In looking at the state of Copyright in Germany, it may be as well to regard first, the general protection given to it throughout the thirty-eight States, composing the Confederation, and afterwards the particular protection afforded to it in each State.

The 18th Article of the Act of the Germanic Confederation, of the date of the 8th of June, 1815, is thus expressed:—

"The Diet shall take into consideration, at its first meeting, some plan for uniform legislation on the liberty of the press, and also what steps are necessary to be taken to secure authors and publishers from invasion of their copyrights."

It appears, that notwithstanding the expediency thus acknowledged, of some measure on the subject, the Diet could not, after frequent deliberations, succeed in coming to any satisfactory conclusion; and matters thus remained until the 6th of September, 1832, when they issued the following decree:—

"In conformity to the 18th article of the Act of the Germanic Confederation, and to preserve the rights of authors, publishers, and booksellers, from piracy of works of literature, or objects of art, the Sovereign Princes and Free Cities of

Germany have resolved to establish as a fundamental principle, that for the future, all distinction with regard to penalties and legal remedies against piracy, between the subjects of one State and the subjects of another, being parties to the Confederation, shall be respectively abolished; so that the publishers, booksellers, and authors of one State, shall enjoy in any other State of the Confederation, the same protection as in that other State shall be enjoyed by its subjects against piracy.

"The most high and high governments will take the necessary measures for the execution of the present decree: they will acquaint the Diet, within two months, as well with the measures they have taken, as with the laws and regulations which exist with regard to piracy."

It would appear, however, that no steps were taken to carry into execution this decree; for we find on the 2nd of April, 1835, another decree issued, which still promises but does not perform.

"The most high and high governments have agreed to prohibit piracy throughout the whole extent of the Confederation, and to establish and secure literary property on uniform principles."

At last, on the 9th of November, 1837, the following resolutions were passed by the Germanic Diet:—

"Art. 1. Literary productions of every kind, as well as works of art, whether already published or not, shall not be multiplied by mechanical means, without the consent of the authors or artists, or those to whom they may have transferred their rights.

"Art. 2. The rights above mentioned shall pass to the heirs or representatives of the authors or artists, or those to whom they have been transferred; and when he who brought out the work, or he who is the editor, is named, this right shall be recognized and protected *in all the States* of the Confederation *for a period of ten years at the least.* This period shall be applicable to literary productions and works of art, which have already appeared within the territories of the Germanic Confederation, during the twenty years which have preceded the date of this resolution, when these productions and works shall be published anew, reckoning from the year of their new publication. When works are published in parts, the period shall be reckoned from the publication of the last part.

"Art. 3 allows the prolonging of the shortest period of Copyright for expensive works for a time not exceeding twenty years.

"Art. 4 gives to authors and artists a right of compensation from all persons, who may publish surreptitious copies of their works, and declares that such surreptitious copies, as well as all the materials used in their production, shall be seized and destroyed.

"Art. 5 interdicts the sale in any of the States of the Confederation of all surreptitious works, whether made within or without the State in which they are offered for sale, and declares that all such sales shall be liable to the penalties of the law.

" Art. 6 requires, that all the States shall communicate to the Diet the measures they shall respectively take for enforcing the observance of the foregoing articles. It also reserves to the Diet the power of deliberating, after the commencement of the year 1842, upon the propriety of extending the term of the rights now granted to literary men and artists, unless circumstances should render an earlier reconsideration of the subject necessary.

" Another separate resolution reserves the question of the rights to be granted to the authors of musical and dramatic works and compositions to future consideration, upon a report about to be made by a commission."

These resolutions were a great boon to authors: for before, a work printed in one State, might have been immediately reprinted in another next adjoining; and the work so reprinted supplied at a cheaper rate to the rest of Germany, than the publisher of the original edition could afford to do. And thus, perhaps, the author of a celebrated work only enjoyed the copyright of it in a small state, whilst it was eagerly sought after and read throughout the vast extent of the Germanic Confederation. But partial measures had been taken, before these resolutions were passed by the Diet, by private treaties, to secure to authors a more extended measure of protection, as we shall find presently in the account of Copyright as it exists in Prussia; and it seems very probable from the state of public feeling on the subject in Germany, that ere long, the duration of the protection thus extended to Copyright throughout the Germanic Confederated States, in addition to that of each particular State where the work is first published, will, in conformity with the tenor of Art. 6, be lengthened, and their rights thus placed on a still firmer and more equitable basis.

I. Austria.

By an imperial ordonnance in 1835, the acts of the Germanic Diet were to extend to every part of the Austrian Empire. The laws respecting Copyright in Austria, are contained in the Code Civil. Art. 1164—1171. *

* A French translation of this code, by A. de Clercq, has been published in the " Coll des lois civ. et crim. des Etats modernes," at the Imprimerie Royale, Paris, 1837.

Art. 1169 declares, that the rights of authors respecting the re-printing of their works *shall not descend to their heirs.*

And Art. 1171 refers to the political laws † *(les lois politiques)* for the penalties to be inflicted in cases of invasion of literary property.

II. Prussia.

This country took an early interest in the protection of Copyright. On the 16th of August, 1827, the king of Prussia addressed to his Minister of State an Order of Council, couched in the following terms :—

" The deliberations of the Diet of Francfort, to arrive at a uniform legislation for the protection of authors and publishers from literary piracies, in conformity to the 18th article of the Act of Confederation, not having been attended with any satisfactory result, I approve of the conclusion of your report of the 23 of July. In consequence of which, and until some definite conclusion shall be arrived at, by a decree of the Diet, negociations shall be entered into with all the German States, in which Copyright is protected, to agree provisionally upon this principle :—that in the application of the existing laws, all distinctions betwixt natives and foreigners shall be abolished as respects the subjects of the contracting States; so that the subjects of one State shall have the same protection in another, as if they were born in the latter. These treaties, when entered into, shall be published in 'the Bulletin des lois.' "

In consequence of this order, treaties for this purpose were concluded, in 1827, 1828, and 1829, with the governments of Anhalt-Bernburg, Anhalt-Dessau, Anhalt-Coethen, Baden, Bavaria, Brunswick, Bremen, Denmark, (as far as regarded the Duchies of Holstein, Lauenburg, and Schleswig,) Hamburg, Hanover, the Grand Duchy of Hesse, and the Electorate of Hesse, Hohenzollern-Hechingen, Hohenzollern-Siegmaringen, Lippe-Detmold, Lübeck, Mecklenburg-Schwerin, Mecklenburg-Strelitz, Nassau, Oldenburg, Reuss-Lobenstein, Reuss-Plau, (the elder branch), Reuss-Schleitz, Saxony, Saxe-Altenburg, Saxe-Coburg, Saxe-Gotha, Saxe-Meiningen, Saxe-Weimar, Schauenburg-Lippe, Schwarzburg-Rudolstadt, Schwarzburg-Sondershausen, Waldeck, and Wurtemberg.

† I have not been able to meet with these laws.

An ordonnance of the King of Prussia, dated the 12th of February, 1833, extended to those provinces of his Kingdom, which do not form part of the Germanic Confederation, the benefits resulting from an uniform system of laws on literary property. This ordonnance is couched in the following terms :

" In the application of the legislative provisions and measures taken with regard to piracies of literary works, and works of art, we abolish all distinction between the subjects of the provinces of our Monarchy, which do not form a part of the Germanic Confederation, and the subjects of the States of that Confederation ; always however on the understanding of reciprocity : therefore the publishers, booksellers, and authors of the Confederated States shall enjoy in our provinces, situated beyond the limits of the Confederation, the same legal protection as is there established, against piratical invasions of their Copyright."

The laws in Prussia, with respect to Copyright, till amended by the law of 1837, were to be found in the 'Code général pour les Etats Prussiens,' partie 1, tit. 11, § 10, 26, et suiv. § 1032 et suiv. partie 2, tit. 20, §. 1294 et suiv : ; a French translation of which was published, 'en l'an IX, à l'imprimerie royale.'

This code treats very largely upon questions arising as to the right of copying or editing works. It would appear from articles 1020, 1021, 1022. 1029, and 1030, that as a general rule, the right of an author did not descend to his heirs, except by an express agreement and in writing : but that even where the right of the author expired for want of such agreement, and every one was free to print his work ; yet if the author had left children in the first remove or degree, the editor, or publisher of the new edition was obliged to make terms with them : so that although the right of editing did not belong to the children of the author, nor could they prevent the reprinting of their parent's works ; yet at least they participated in the profit gained by booksellers, in their re-impression.

But now by an ordonnance of the date of the 11th of July, 1837, the law of Copyright throughout Prussia, is put on a more favourable and juster basis.

Sect. 5 declares that an author shall enjoy the sole right of printing his work *for his life*.

Sect. 6 confers on the heirs of the author the same right *for a period of thirty years*, to be reckoned *from his death* : the same in the case of a posthumous publication as in any other: and that after that period every work shall be open to any to print.

Sect. 35 gives a retrospective effect to the foregoing clauses.

And Sect. 38 extends the protection of this law to works first published in a foreign state, in the same proportion as works first published in Prussia are protected in that foreign state.

A project of a law has been lately prepared by the government of Prussia, to prevent the introduction into Germany of piratical editions of German works printed abroad, in France, Belgium, and Switzerland; which up to this time was not prohibited by any legislative enactments: and this law was to be submitted for adoption to the rest of the Germanic States.

III. Bavaria.

The Code civil of Bavaria, which contains the regulations for the protection of Copyright in that country, has not yet been published; but it would appear from the terms of the following article of the Code penal, that literary property descends to the heir or representative of the author in that country; but for how long, does not appear.

Art. 397. "The regulations relative to the protection which literary property enjoys, are contained in the Code civil. Every person who shall, without the consent of the author, *his heirs, or representatives*, publish by printing or otherwise, a work of science or art, without having so altered it as to make it a work of his own, shall be liable, independently of a claim for damages, to the penalties contained in the privileges accorded to publishers; or where there are no particular penalties enjoined, then to the punishments established by the law relative to offences against the police.

IV. Wurtemberg.

In Wurtemberg, an ordonnance of the date of the 21st of February, 1815, prohibited any from reprinting a work, the sole printing of which had been granted by a privilege from the King.

On the 11th of July, 1836, was presented to the Chamber of Deputies, the following project of a provisional law on Copyright.

'Until a general law can be made with respect to literary property, the following regulations shall be observed: Art. 1. Authors and publishers, subjects of one of the Germanic States, shall enjoy, with respect to all works already printed or hereafter to be printed, the sole right of re-printing them *for six years from their first publication,* without any payment, and with the same protection against piracy, as if they had obtained a special privilege, in conformity to the law of the 21st of Feb. 1815. Art. 2 permits unauthorized copies already printed at the passing of this law, to be sold, on bringing them to be stamped within a month after the passing of the law, for which no charge shall be made. Art. 3 saves the rights of all those, who under the existing law enjoy a more extensive privilege than would be conferred on them by this law.'

This law was passed on the 22nd of July, 1836.

V. Baden.

The law of Literary Property in the Grand Duchy of Baden, forms eight additional articles to the title "Propriété" in the Code civil;* and from them, it would appear that an author's right to the sole reprinting of his works *descends to his heirs,* and is not extinguished by his death; unless he has parted with his interest to a publisher; when it is open to all to print, if the bookseller has not obtained a special privilege.†

VI. Hesse-Cassel.

In Hesse Cassel an ordinance has been published, that after the 1st of July, 1829, no work first printed and published in a state of the Germanic Confederation, where the author, printer, and publisher, reside in the state where it is published, shall be reprinted within the

* Art. 577, d-a- to 577, d-h-

† I am not sure that the above is the correct construction of these articles: for I have only been able to meet with them in a French translation, and any inference that may be drawn from the use of one word instead of another, is, when applied to a translation, liable to great error.

Electorate of Hesse, *during the life time* of the author, or *for a term of ten years after his decease* : provided that in such State, where the work is first published, copyright be acknowledged and protected.

VII. Saxe-Coburg-Gotha.

In this Duchy, an ordinance has also been published (in 1827), against literary piracy. It directs that after *thirty years* have elapsed *from the death* of an author, all rights that have descended to his heirs shall cease, as well as those which have been acquired by booksellers.

VIII. Saxe-Meiningen.

An ordonnance of the Duke of Saxe-Meiningen, of the date of the 23rd of April, 1829, declares the duration of Copyright to be *for the life* of the author, and *for twenty years after his death.*

IX. Hamburgh.

The Senate published, in July 1828, a provisionary decree for the protection of literary property, till the Diet should determine the question finally, giving the exclusive privilege of reprinting, *for two years,* within the city and its territory, to all works first printed in one of the States of the Confederation : such term to date from the date of publication.

X. Other States.

In *Saxony,* an edict of 1773 prohibits literary piracy ; in *Hanover,* one of the 17th of September, 1827 ; in *Nassau,* one of the 4th and 5th of March, 1814 ; in *Reuss,* one of the 24th of December, 1827 ; and in *Anhalt-Coethen,* one of 1829 ; but I am not able to state the periods for which Copyright endures in these countries. Enough, however, has been shown, to prove that the greater part of Germany is favourable to the principle, *which extends the property in a work for a certain period beyond the death of the author for the benefit of his heirs;* and it must not be forgotten that, independent of the peculiar privileges which an author enjoys in his own State, he participates in the benefit of the Act of the diet of 1837, which gives him an exclusive privilege over a vast tract of country, comprising many independent kingdoms and principalities, speaking the same common language, for the space of ten years; and that there is great probability that ere long even this term will be increased.

RUSSIA.

When we come to look at the Russian laws, we find an enlightened liberality of conduct with regard to the rights and privileges of authors, which should make governments that boast of more freedom and civilization, shrink from the comparison.

In the Russian Code, we shall find what is not to be found in any other state, an enactment conferring on certain degrees of literary success, certain titles of rank and honour;* and although I may be told, that without the ostentatious formality of a law to that effect, other nations confer as substantial and as flattering marks of distinction on their men of genius and learning,—I will answer, that yet it cannot fail to be a favourable sign of the legislation of a country, when the claims of genius and learning to an honourable situation are thus publicly acknowledged and secured by the statutes of the country which they enlighten and adorn. But this is not the proper place to discuss this question, our object now being to show the difference in the protection afforded to Copyright under different governments.

A law passed in January, 1830, repealed a former law on the 4th of May, 1828, and enjoins the following provisions, which form the present law on the subject.

The author or translator of a work shall have the sole right of printing and disposing of it *during his lifetime,* and his heirs and assigns shall enjoy the same *for the term of twenty-five years after his de-*

* See the extracts given in the Rev. Etr. de Legisl. tom. iv.

cease; and for a *further term of ten years,* if they shall publish an edition within five years before the expiration of the first term.

The Copyright of a work which the author has not parted with, cannot be taken in execution by his creditors, no matter whether it has been published or not; nor in cases of bankruptcy of booksellers, can the creditors avail themselves of any benefit to which the bookseller might have been entitled by any contract with an author, unless they fulfil the same engagements with the author which the bankrupt had bound himself to perform.

In every case, the party guilty of piracy shall pay to the proprietor of the work the difference between the actual cost of the pirated edition, and the selling price of the original edition; and shall forfeit to the use of the proprietor all the copies of such unlawful reprint. And until definitive judgment shall be pronounced, the edition accused of being pirated shall be restrained from being sold. The judgment shall determine the amount of damages resulting from the offence.

Such is a brief outline of the present law of Copyright in Russia, which, for the protection it affords literary property, may safely challenge comparison with the legislative enactments of most countries in Europe.

DENMARK.

Mr. Nicklin, the American bookseller, in his little pamphlet on Literary Property, Pref. p. vi., says that he had the following information "from the best authority." "The Copyright of publications in Denmark is *perpetual.* The reprinting of foreign works is generally permitted, with the exception of those of foreign countries protected by treaty stipulations, to which Denmark more particularly has acceded with the German States." As to the treaty stipulations, see ante p. 124, by which it appears that they only apply to the Duchies of Holstein, Lauenburg, and Schleswig.

NORWAY AND SWEDEN.

"In these countries," says a learned writer, in the Amer. Jurist. vol. x, p. 69, "the Copyright is *perpetual.*"

SPAIN.

Victor Foucher is of opinion that the proper construction to be put upon a law of 1805, is, that Copyright is *perpetual* in this country. He refers to "Novissima Recopilatione, 1805, liv. 8, tit. 15, 16, 17, 18, and 19." *

THE TWO SICILIES.

Articles 322 and 323 of the penal code of the Kingdom of the Two Sicilies, † punish literary piracy with a fine of not less than one third, nor more than the double of the sum awarded as damages to the proprietor of the Copyright, two thirds of which fine are to go in addition to damages and the confiscated copies to the proprietor; and besides these punishments, imprisonment for one month is added when the damages exceed 500 ducats (£85).

Respecting the duration of Copyright, and the privileges of authors, Victor Foucher says, "that although he is not able to affirm it, he believes that they are *the same as in France*, the Sicilies having retained, as he understands, the 'lois civiles' of that country. ‡

* Rev. Etr. de Legisl. tom. iv. p. 370, *bis.*

† There is a French translation of this code in the 'Coll. des lois civ. et crim. des Etats Modernes' — A l'imprim. Roy. Paris, 1834—7.

‡ Rev. Etr. de Legisl. tom. iv. p. 370, *bis.*

PRINTED BY J. GREEN AND CO., BARTLETT'S BUILDINGS.